DEDICATION

*To the greatest horses of all time —
the ones that teach.*

ACKNOWLEDGMENTS

*A lot of people helped to make the photos in this book possible.
Thanks to the staff and students at Woodland Horse Center in
Silver Spring, Maryland, especially Tammy and Kate Gildea. A
special thanks to Jane Seigler and Hank Huston of Reddemeade
Horse Center in Silver Spring for their time and efforts.*

Contents

Introduction

"I CAN RIDE."

How many times in the past 25 years have I heard this from aspiring riders? What they meant to say was, "I once sat on a horse." Some of them venture to add something like, "The horse ate grass and wouldn't move," or "It ran me under a tree, threw me, and then took off for the barn."

Riding is a sport and an art. There's a lot more to it than just sitting on a horse and steering it around. To learn to ride really well, you need a few key attributes:

- Although you don't have to be a trained athlete, you do need to be relatively physically fit.
- You need dedication, which means you're willing to devote time and to pay some money for riding lessons.
- You need compassion for horses; a combative attitude won't get you far.
- You also need to understand the horse or at least be interested in learning about him.
- A horse is instinctive, but doesn't always just react — he uses his brain. You need to know that when you approach a horse, you're entering his territory.

To help students understand what riding is all about, I like to contrast it to playing tennis. In tennis, you have a court of uniform size, a racquet, and a ball, and the net is always the same height. It's not easy to play tennis well, but you're more or less in control. If you hit the ball with the racquet exactly the same way and all other conditions remain constant, the ball will land in the same place. Why? Neither the racquet nor the ball thinks. But a horse does. On one day, you'll give him an aid — a cue to move a certain way — and he'll go to the right, but the next day you may do the same thing and he'll go left. The horse processes everything he perceives around him, not just the aids you give. Remember, he has a brain, and he uses it.

Riding means learning to work in sync with the horse, to handle these variable conditions and responses, and to convince the horse to do what you want with some consistency. You work in harmony with a powerful, unique thinking animal.

I caution students not to forget why most of us ride: for recreation and to escape the pressures of daily life. I believe that instructors should strive to make riding fun for their students, but you should nevertheless expect to meet stumbling blocks along the way. Learn to take them, ahem, in stride.

One of the most common frustrations new riders face occurs when their minds outpace their bodies. Don't give up. You *can* master the skills you need. If you maintain your interest and get past the pitfalls, you'll find riding both challenging and exciting. In the end, you'll get back far more from the expereince than the effort you put in.

How to Use This Book

This book is a *companion guide to riding lessons,* not a teach-yourself-to-ride manual.

Writing a book about learning to ride is a risky business because there are so many schools of thought on the subject. This book deals with English riding. (That's the type of riding you do on a saddle without a horn.) The principles of riding are the same for English and Western (the other basic style of riding), with minor differences in the aids. Most instructors find that it is easier to teach an English rider Western riding than it is to teach a Western rider English riding. That's why this book is geared to beginning English riders.

I teach balance seat. There are many different seats: hunt seat, stock seat, saddle seat, to name a few. The balance seat can be described as riding on balance as opposed to gripping. It is the oldest of all seats and is the basis of all other seats. The methods I discuss in this book are those that I use. But I certainly don't believe my way is the only way. The last thing an instructor trying to teach a new skill wants to hear from a student is, "But I read in a book that it should be done this way." If I tell you something that contradicts what your instructor tells you, *listen to your riding instructor.* I'm not there, I didn't train the horse, nor do I know you. So do what your riding instructor recommends.

A riding instructor can provide direction and demonstrations that often will help you understand a skill much faster than reading about it and trying it yourself. A good riding instructor also will help ensure your safety while you learn to ride. All in all, you're going to get a lot from your riding instructor that you cannot get from a book.

What this book *will* do is help you get the most out of the riding lessons that you take at a reputable stable from qualified instructors.

I'll be discussing riding skills in the order I prefer to teach them, but you don't necessarily have to follow this sequence. Your instructor may choose a different order, and with good reason. Moreover, don't expect to absorb everything I cover in one chapter during one riding lesson. Some chapters may take you several lessons. Let your instructor determine the learning pace, which varies widely among instructors and students.

Use this book to complement and reinforce what you learn in riding classes. Use it to help you answer such questions as "What the devil did my instructor say an 'aid' was?" Use it to learn your way around the barn, to learn about horses, and to enjoy riding.

One last word. Each chapter profiles a different horse. Although some of the facts have been changed for learning purposes, the profiles are mostly based on real horses from one of my barns, Woodland Horse Center in Silver Spring, Maryland. You'll learn from these profiles that horses are as individual as people, and from this book that one of the great joys of learning to ride is meeting and working with the best horses of all time — the horses that teach you. That's why I've dedicated this book to them.

THE BASICS

PART I

 **Lesson** **1**

Leading, Mounting, and Walking

DURING THE MORE THAN 20 YEARS I've been teaching (and no, I'm not old!), one thing I've learned is that people who sign up for riding instruction want to hurry up and get on the horse. This chapter should give you a real feel for what that first riding lesson entails.

Safety advice is built into all the lessons, but check out the especially important rules at the end of this lesson (page 21). Above all, wear a safety helmet; a good lesson barn will make sure you wear one. For more detailed information about what to wear during your riding lesson, see the box at the end of lesson 3 (page 41).

I'm assuming that since you're a beginner, the stable has tacked up a suitable school horse for you, one that's kind, calm, and patient. She should be a horse something like Sprite.

Sprite

AGE: 20   BREED: Quarter Horse
WEIGHT: Not telling   COLOR: Black
SIZE: 14.3 hands

Sprite is a small, stocky, sturdy, cute horse. If she were any shorter, she'd be a pony. In the winter, her coat gets very long and she looks like a wooly mammoth. She's sassy in the field, and you can tell she was hot stuff in her younger years. Now that she's getting a little older, she has to watch what she eats.

Sprite's also the motherly type. She babysits horses that don't like to stay alone in the barn or pasture. She stands nice and still when a new student mounts, although she might move if you jab her with a knee or toe. A terrific trail horse, Sprite proudly leads where other horses fear to venture. Being calm and trustworthy makes her a good confidence builder for the beginning rider.

Leading the Horse

Sprite stands in her stall with saddle pad, saddle, girth, and bridle on. Your first task is to lead her from the stall to the ring for your lesson. Make sure your riding helmet is on and fastened securely.

Now here you go, into the stall. Sprite sees you. She's smiling, with the faintest twinkle in her eyes. Her ears are up. She seems really friendly.

Does she know you're a beginner? You bet. Horses can read body language. After all, that's their main method of communicating with other horses. You're acting a bit timid, and that's how she knows you're a novice.

The next five minutes will largely determine how your horse behaves during the riding lesson. If you know what to do and act with self-assurance, the horse will be more likely to cooperate. *Stand up there and have confidence!*

Always work from the horse's left side, which is what she's been trained to expect. Stand facing Sprite's left shoulder and gently but confidently lift the reins off her neck and bring them over her head. It's a good idea to talk to her in a calm, friendly voice. Continue to stand at her left shoulder, but now face forward — the same way Sprite is facing.

With your right hand, hold both reins about four or five inches below the bit, under Sprite's chin. Gather the surplus reins in your left hand, being sure not to let the ends drag or droop. You certainly don't want to trip on them, and if Sprite steps on them, she could panic and rear back. Don't loop the reins around your arm or hand.

Horses are led with the reins off their necks and under their chin so that if something untoward happens, heaven forbid, you can quickly move away from the horse. You can't do this if the reins are still on the horse's neck and you're holding them just under the chin.

Despite what you've seen in the movies, you should *never* tie the horse's reins to anything. John Wayne may have ridden up to the saloon, tied his horse to the hitching rail, and sauntered into the saloon for a drink, but if a tied horse panics and pulls hard, she could seriously injure her lower jaw.

Open the stall door *all the way*. Otherwise, the horse could bang her hips as you lead her through. Make sure you close or push aside the latches, locks, or anything else that might jab her in the side. You don't want to start your first lesson on a horse that holds a grudge. You also don't want the saddle to get torn (saddles are very expensive).

Warm-up

It's always a good idea to get your blood flowing and warm up your muscles before doing any kind of exercise, including riding. Take a walk around the block, run up and down a stairway, or jog in place. Then stretch out to help you limber up and prevent soreness after your riding lesson.

The following stretches can be done before class at the barn, after five minutes of warm-up activity, such as walking. To keep strain off your back, place your feet hip-width apart, bend your knees slightly, and hold in your abdominal muscles. Repeat each of the following four times before moving on to the next, holding each move for a count of ten.

- Reach way up over your head with both hands. Reach higher with the left hand, then the right.

- With arms stretched out on either side, twist gently left, then right.

- With hands on hips, bend sideways to the left, then to the right.

- With hands on hips, bend forward from the waist, then backward as far as you comfortably can.

▶

*Always position
yourself at the horse's
left shoulder, and look
where you're going, not
at the horse's feet.*

Now step ahead of Sprite to lead her out, since the two of you can't get through most stall doors at the same time, and then resume your position at her left shoulder as you walk with her.

Look where *you* are going, not at the horse's feet. You'd be surprised how easy it is to walk into something.

Even with the best of planning, a few things can go wrong. Don't worry, you can fix them.

What to do if . . . the horse won't move.

Don't try to drag her by the reins. Most horses weigh nearly half a ton or more. You're not going to drag her anywhere.

Try a little cluck with your tongue or a gentle tap on the shoulder to get her going. If that doesn't work, ask for help. Barns generally are full of friendly people who will gladly help you out. Don't be afraid to ask.

Once out of the barn, your horse stops again. If she refuses to move, simply use the reins to turn her to the left or right a bit until she has to take a step, and then walk forward. You control horses not by overpowering them but by changing their thought process. That's why turning them left or right will get them going. *Turn* your horse back in the direction you want to go. Remember, never try to *drag* a horse anywhere.

What to do if . . . the horse seems to be chasing you.

She isn't really. Beginners are usually unsure of themselves and tend to stand too far from the horse. As a result, she follows you, moving closer and closer, until you're convinced she's chasing you. But try to remember that you're *leading* her, she's not chasing you. Walk where you want to go, next to your horse's left shoulder.

***What to do if . . . the horse puts down her head, eats grass,
and won't budge.***

> Prevent the horse from getting to grass in the first place. But if she's
> already there, try to turn her away with the reins. Step away to get her
> head up.
>
> This time when you lead her, keep her head a little higher than she
> wants it — at about your shoulder height — so she doesn't have a
> chance to get to the grass. If you let her carry her head well below her
> shoulder, she can grab that grass before you can respond.

What to do if . . . the horse is pulling you.

> Give a little *check* with the reins. Just make a sharp upward, snapping
> motion. That's a check. Steady pulls don't work with a horse. (Note:
> Before you give a check, there should be a little slack in the reins). The
> check should tell her to slow down. If that doesn't do it, try again, more
> firmly. Let the horse know that you're in control and that she must
> walk at the pace you dictate.

Leading a Horse out of the Barn

1. Make sure your riding helmet is on.
2. Lift the reins off the horse's neck and forward over her head, and
   carry them under her chin so they don't drag.
3. Stand on the horse's left side.
4. Keep the horse's head a little above shoulder height.
5. Open the stall door all the way; make sure latches are pushed back
   or in.
6. Walk in front of the horse to get her out the door.
7. Resume your position close to the horse's left shoulder.
8. Give a little tug up with the reins to remind her she's not going to eat
   the grass ahead.

Mounting the Horse

Well, you've finally gotten Sprite into the ring. If you're taking group
lessons, stay away from other horses. Now, before you mount, there are a
few things you must do. First, look to see that Sprite's saddle pad isn't
bunched or folded up and that the bridle, reins, and stirrup leathers don't
have any obvious torn or weak places that could present a safety hazard.

Checking the Girth

The **girth** is the strap that goes under the horse's belly and connects to
both sides of the saddle. You should just be able to slide your flat hand
between the girth and the horse. If you can make a fist between the girth
and the horse, the girth is too loose.

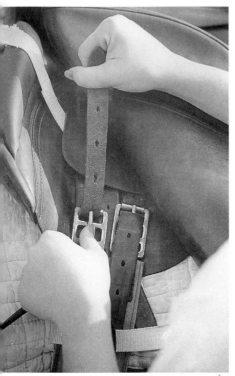

Raise the flap on the left side of the saddle, and find the two buckles at the end of the girth. They are attached to lengths of leather called **billets.** Tighten each buckle *one hole at a time* — first one buckle, then the other, then repeat — until the girth is tight enough. If you crank up more than one hole at a time, you could cause your horse discomfort, and she might retaliate with a nip.

Notice that there are three billets on an **English saddle.** You always want to use the first billet, that is, the one closest to the horse's head, and the second *or* third billet. (Generally, the girths commonly used today fit best if you use the first and third billets.) The first billet is attached to the saddle differently than the others and is called a safety billet. If the second or third billet breaks, the first billet should still hold the saddle in place.

Adjusting the Stirrups

You put your feet in the **stirrup irons** when you're in the saddle. Strips of leather called **stirrup leathers** hold them in place. The stirrup irons should be "run up" — pushed up to the top of the stirrup leathers, resting just under the saddle flap — when you lead an unmounted horse. This prevents the irons from banging the horse in her sides or getting caught in something while you're leading. To mount, you'll need to pull the **stirrups** down and then adjust them to the proper length using the buckle on each side.

▲
To secure the girth, tighten each buckle one hole at a time until you can slide only your flat hand between the girth and the horse.

Parts of the English Saddle

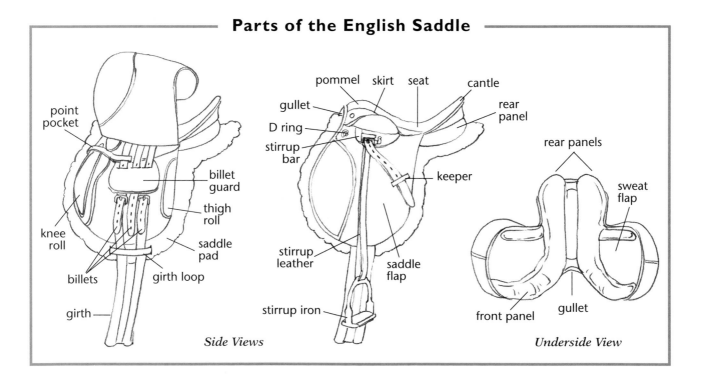

Side Views

Underside View

To approximate the proper stirrup length, place the tip of your fingers against the **stirrup bar** of the saddle. You'll find it under the saddle flap; it's the metal piece where the stirrup leathers are attached. Lift the stirrup to your armpit. If it doesn't reach your armpit, lengthen the stirrup leathers; if there's slack in the stirrup leathers, shorten them. This is only a general guide, however, for mounting. Your instructor may very well want to readjust your stirrup length once you're up in the saddle.

◀

A proper stirrup length should be approximately the distance from your armpit to your fingertips.

Holding the Reins for Mounting

Bring the horse's reins over her head and neck. Hold the reins in your left hand, and shorten the off rein — the rein on the *other* side of the horse — just a bit. The **off side** is always the right side of the horse. (The left side is always the **near side**.) You want the off rein shorter so that the horse's head is turned slightly away from you. This will prevent the horse from being able to bite you. Most good beginner school horses won't bite, but you want to form good habits from the beginning. A bite in the butt hurts like the dickens, but it's nothing compared to the embarrassment you'll feel in the emergency room when you explain what happened.

There's one other reason to hold the reins this way. If your horse moves, she'll walk into you, which can make it easier for you to mount. It also tends to stop a horse from backing up while you're mounting.

Getting On

With your left hand grasping the reins, also grab *a lot* of mane in the same hand. This does not hurt the horse; horses have minimal sensitivity in their manes.

Bring up your left foot and place it into the stirrup. Oh no! You can't lift your foot that high? Try this: Stand at Sprite's shoulder, facing her rear. Lean forward and grab the top of the stirrup iron with your right hand. Lean back while continuing to hold onto the mane with your left hand (**a**). As you lean back, your left foot comes up. Place the stirrup on your foot (**b**).

Now turn so your shoulders are square to the side of the saddle. Your left knee should be pointing toward Sprite's nose. Hold the back of the saddle (the **_cantle_**) on the off side with your right hand, resting your wrist on the saddle seat (**c**). Spring from your right foot and push down with your hands while swinging your right leg over. As you spring up, your upper body should go _across_ the horse, not straight up in the air, which can make the saddle slip to the side (**d**). Now, gently sit down in the saddle.

▶
To mount a horse, first grab the reins and mane in your left hand and hold the stirrup in your right (a). Then lean back slightly to put your left foot in the stirrup (b).

▶
Holding onto the saddle with your right hand, spring up from your right foot and lean across the horse (c). Swing your right leg over the horse's rump (d).

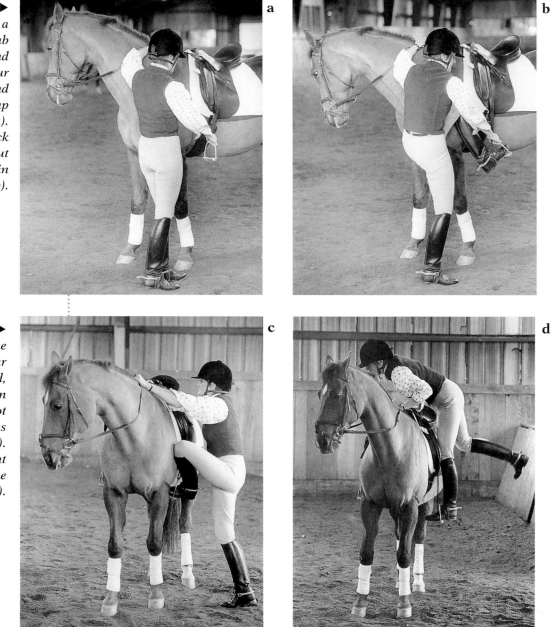

Here's an extra tip or two: Instead of *pulling* with your arms as you get onto the saddle, *push down* as you boost yourself up; straighten your left leg somewhat as you come up. Don't forget to let go of the back of the saddle with your right hand as you swing your right leg over.

Keep in mind that riding should be fun, but learning to ride is a complex process. You're bound to make mistakes. Don't hesitate to laugh at yourself and smile at others along the way.

Before proceeding, you should look at some of the problems that commonly occur while mounting and what you can do about them.

What to do if . . . the horse won't stand still.

A good school horse should be trained to stand still for mounting, but even a well-behaved horse will fidget from time to time or try to walk off. The most expedient and safest solution is to ask for help. Your instructor or an assistant can hold the horse while you mount. Never hesitate to ask for help.

Do not continue to try to mount alone if the horse won't stand still. You don't want to risk having one foot in the stirrup and the other on the ground as a horse walks off, because it's hard to hop along at four miles an hour with one foot up in the air.

What to do if . . . the saddle slips when you put weight on the stirrup.

Your girth isn't tight enough. You checked it? Well, some horses are very clever at tensing their muscles while the girth is being fastened. Then they relax, and guess what? The girth is slack. So recheck the girth as you get ready to mount, several times if necessary. Tighten it up one hole at a time.

If, however, the girth is tight and the saddle still slips, you may be trying to mount by going straight up into the air instead of across the horse's back. The secret is to get your body mass centered over the horse. You might also be trying to pull yourself up instead of pushing down with your arms.

Why Not Use a Mounting Block?

Many riders use a **mounting block**, which is a box or stepping stool that makes it easier to reach the stirrup and mount the horse. If you're a very short person riding a very tall horse, a mounting block will be necessary. Generally, however, beginning riders are assigned a horse that isn't so tall.

I believe that if you're going to ride, you should learn how to get up on a horse without a mounting block. If you can't, what will you do if you must dismount and then mount again where you don't have something to stand on? Now is the time to learn to mount. Once you've mastered this skill, it's okay to use a mounting block. In fact, in some cases, it's preferable; compared to mounting from the ground, mounting from a block causes less torque on the girth and the horse's middle. But always maintain your ability to mount without a block.

Holding the Reins Correctly

Before you ride, you've got to know how to hold the reins. The first three fingers of each hand (starting with the index finger, not the thumb) go over the rein, and the rein comes out between the third and fourth (or little) finger. Later in the book, you'll learn more about how to use your hands, but for now just gently close your fingers around the reins. Don't use a death grip. Your hands should be relaxed.

Keep both thumbs up, pressing against the reins and your forefingers. The fingernails on each hand should face each other, about four inches apart. Hold your hands about two inches above the horse's *withers* (the ridge between the shoulder bones); see photograph below.

To hold the reins correctly, position your first three fingers over the rein and the fourth under it.

Avoid slack reins, but don't hold them so tightly that they pull back on the horse. Keep steady contact between your hands and the horse's mouth; through the reins, the horse's mouth should feel elastic.

The Rider's Position

To stay balanced on the horse, you've got to sit correctly. A straight line should connect your ear, shoulder, hip, and heel. Aligning your upper and lower body in this way is referred to as positioning your legs ***at the girth*** and helps you connect with your horse's center balance. From the top down:

✓ Your head faces forward.

✓ Your tongue is in your mouth, not sticking out between your teeth.

✓ Your shoulders are relaxed, back and down.

✓ Your elbows lightly hug your sides.

✓ Your hands hold the reins correctly (as described above).

✓ Your hips are relaxed so they can follow the horse's motion.

✓ Your thighs and knees point down as much as possible. They should not grip, but rest lightly against the horse. You should feel as though you're kneeling, more than sitting.

✓ Your upper calves rest against the horse.

✓ Your heels are lower than your toes.

✓ Your toes point in the general direction you're traveling.

As you can see, learning to ride requires you to remember a lot at once, but it will come with practice.

◀

The correct rider position requires that your ear, shoulder, hip, and heel are aligned.

Asking the Horse to Move Forward

Notice I've used the word "ask" instead of "make," because you can't make the horse do anything, especially at the beginner stage. You ask, and hope the horse helps out.

To ask the horse to move forward, sit down in your seat, pull both legs back about two inches, and **pulse** — squeeze and release— simultaneously with both lower legs. At the same time, push forward with your back.

Think of sitting on a horse as being like sitting on a swing with your feet off the ground. You want to make the swing move, so you push with your back. You also **give** with your hands, which means you release the tension in the reins slightly. Yes, there's a lot to do at once!

Once the horse begins moving, both your legs should return to their normal position: heels in line with your hips and shoulders. The hands reestablish light, elastic contact with the horse's mouth.

Caution: Most beginners hold their reins with too much slack. If you can't affect the horse without lifting your hands or moving them to the side or behind your hips, your reins are too long.

All these messages you're sending the horse are called *aids*. To summarize, here are the aids that ask the horse to walk:

Aids to the Walk

1. Sit down.
2. Squeeze *evenly* with both your lower legs to encourage the horse to keep moving.
3. Push with your back.
4. Give with your hands.

To keep Sprite walking or to encourage her to walk faster, squeeze with your right and left legs *alternately*. She's been trained to specific sets of stimuli. If you squeeze your legs simultaneously, you're giving a different command. If you stop using your legs, your horse will slow down or stop.

Now walk around a little bit and see how this feels. Wow! It feels pretty good! So try walking a little faster.

Please note that when I say squeeze with your *legs,* I mean your *calves*. With a slow school horse, you may have to use your heels, too, to start her moving, but always try first with your calves. I'm not criticizing school horses, because they'll keep you safe while you're learning, but they may require some extra encouragement.

What to do if . . . the horse walks but not in a straight line.

Chances are you forgot to think about where you're going. Remember, you're thinking for two, and maybe you aren't giving completely clear signals. Pick something straight ahead to aim for, such as a post in the

Gaits and Beats

Walking — like trotting and cantering — is a kind of *gait*, or way in which the horse moves forward. Each gait is distinguished by its sequence of leg movements. The walk, shown below, is a four-beat gait. The trot is a two-beat gait, and the canter, a three-beat gait. A *beat* is when one or more of the horse's feet hit the ground. When walking, a horse places each of her four feet on the ground separately; thus the walk is a four-beat gait.

1   2   3   4

fence. Focus on that spot as you ask her to move forward. By giving yourself direction, you'll give your horse direction, too.

What to do if . . .the horse walks faster than you want her to.

First figure out why. Is another horse on the other side of the ring? If so, your horse is probably following her herd instinct. Is the other horse swishing his tail? That means he might kick.

Maybe the gate to the ring is open and Sprite has decided that she's had it with the greenhorn on her back and that it's time to go back to her stall. But you can't let her, because your lesson's not over.

My point is that you must maintain control. Do not let any horse you are riding get too close to other horses. Stay several horse lengths apart unless instructed to do otherwise. You must tell your horse that she has to help you complete your riding lesson. She must go where you tell her to go.

What to do if . . . the horse just won't move forward.

This requires an approach similar to the one you use when you're leading a horse and she stops — namely, try a different tactic. It's important that the horse always does what you say, but how you tell her to do what you want is equally important. If the horse doesn't respond the first time you give an aid, and if you're pretty certain you gave the aid correctly, apply the aid (or aids) again, but more harshly. Learning to apply aids more harshly is an important skill, and it's called the *progression of the aids*.

It's unlikely you'll fail using the aids progressively. I want to make another point here. Kicking a horse is not necessarily bad if you do it as part of a progression. You will never have my permission to kick hard if it isn't. (Imagine being beaten every time you fail to respond appropriately or fast enough to someone's request. Maybe you didn't even hear the request.)

Progression of Leg Aids

The progression of the aids will prove invaluable to you as your riding progresses, so study this skill carefully. Here's a simplified version:

1. Squeeze with lower legs/upper calves.
2. If no response: Kick lightly with your heels.
3. If no response: Kick hard with your heels.
4. If no response: Give several sharp kicks with your heels.
5. If you still get no response, you'll probably need a crop, which you'll learn about in lesson 2.

Now that you've got Sprite walking, see if you can stop her, which is known in the horse world as a **halt**.

Halting the Horse

To stop, or halt, the horse, you stop following the horse with your seat and you *set* your hands. This means that you set your hands in one spot and apply steady, even pressure on the bit with both reins, but without pulling back. Simultaneously, gently close your legs on the horse while stiffening your back a bit.

Aids to the Halt

1. Sit down (or stop following the horse with your seat).
2. Set your hands (you do not give to the horse with the reins).
3. Gently close your calves on the horse.
4. Stiffen your back.

What to do if . . . the horse won't stop.

So far I've given you the textbook version of a halt. It's the way a halt should be done, and it's the way you should first try to halt. But you must also maintain control of your horse, so if the textbook version doesn't work, pull back on the reins. Tell the horse to stop — not verbally, but with progressive severity of your aids.

What to do if . . . the horse backs up when you ask her to stop.

If you don't release the pressure on the bit after you stop, Sprite will start backing up. In fact, that's how she's trained to back up. Move your hands forward just an inch or two to release the pressure on the bit, and apply slight pressure with both your lower legs, just enough to tell her not to back up.

It takes practice and finesse to achieve just the right pressure with your hands and your legs. Whatever you do, don't panic and pull back on the reins even more.

As soon as the horse stops, release any pressure on the reins. That's the horse's reward for stopping. Once the horse halts, relax. Look around and smell the roses. Practice walking several strides, then stop for several seconds, walk again, and stop again.

Walking Faster

There are different types of walks, but for now you should simply practice walking faster, which riders sometimes refer to as adding **impulsion** to the walk. To do this, use the same basic aids for the walk but apply them with more insistence.

Start your horse walking as you did before, and then let her know you want her to go faster by squeezing with the left leg, then the right, the left, the right, and so forth. Use your back more dramatically. The farther back your legs are, the more aggressive the signal to the horse.

Aids to Add Impulsion to the Walk

1. Squeeze with alternate legs — pulse with one leg, then the other, as much as you need to achieve the desired speed.
2. Follow the horse with your seat and back a bit more intensely. This encourages the horse to lengthen her stride.

    You should already have given with your hands when you first asked Sprite to walk, but your reins shouldn't become too slack.

This is great, isn't it? Is the wind blowing your hair and flapping your cheeks? Well, maybe you're not going quite that fast, but you're moving right along. Next, why not try a turn?

Turning Left or Right

To turn left, *close* your left hand, or pull gently on the left rein, and give with your right hand by moving it very slightly forward. However much you pull on the left rein, you should give equally with your right. You reverse this process to turn right.

Alas, you try this maneuver and nothing happens! Sprite turns her head and stares at you with those big brown eyes, a blank look on her face. Here's the problem: You used a rein without using your legs. Sprite did exactly what you asked her to do: She turned her head. Something has to tell her to move forward and turn her body too, and that's your legs. Try this:

Aids to Turning Left

1. Close your left hand.
2. Give with your right hand.
3. Pivot your shoulders and head slightly left.
4. Squeeze and release with your inside (left) leg.
5. Keep your right, or outside, leg about two inches behind the girth.
   To turn right, close the right hand, give with the left hand, and so forth.

Riding and controlling the horse is nothing more than using pressure to issue subtle commands. You vary the balance of pressure from your hands and legs to bring about the desired result. You never use a hand without using a leg.

If this textbook version of how to turn isn't working, or you're getting confused trying to coordinate your hand and leg aids, try this to turn left:

Alternative Aids to Turning Left

1. Pull on the left rein.
2. Squeeze with both legs.

Walk straight for several steps, and turn left again. Next, practice turning right.

Now try alternating turns. Walk about 10 strides, then ask your horse to turn right. Walk another 10 strides, then ask her to turn left.

Try making a complete circle to the left. First, visualize a circle about 60 feet in diameter. Focus on it. Ask your horse to walk, then turn gradually onto the circumference of the circle. Once you've successfully completed a circle to the left, try a circle to the right.

What to do if . . . the horse slows down or stops when you ask her to turn.

You may not have followed your hand aids with the leg aids soon enough. Understand that in all instances pulling back on the reins — even when you only pull with one hand — means "stop" or "slow down" to the horse. Something must also say to the horse, "No, don't stop or slow down, but *turn*." That something is the pulse from your leg.

You may be squeezing continuously, with the horse unable to feel the difference in pressure. Or you might be squeezing with your knee or thighs instead of your lower legs. So squeeze with the inside of your calves and then release. If you grip constantly, you'll never communicate with your horse; it's like trying to talk while holding your lips stiffly.

The horse might also fail to turn if you give too sharp a signal with the rein. This would cause her to lose her energy, or impulsion. Never pull a horse's head so far to the side that it moves beyond her shoulder.

Last but not least, many beginners try to turn left by pushing both hands to the left side of the horse's withers. It's an especially common problem among those who have ridden before without the benefit of lessons.

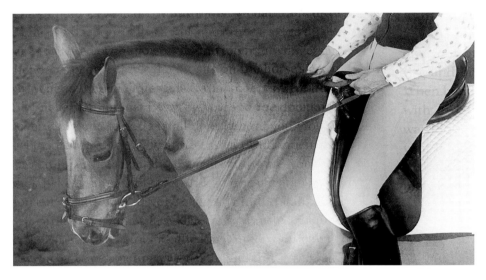

◀
To turn left, pull gently on, or close, the left rein and give, or yield, the same amount with the right rein.

What to do if . . . you asked the horse correctly, but she refuses to turn.

This is a serious problem. It will feel like you're driving a truck without power steering. If your horse is following another horse, she simply may not want to turn away from him. Put more space, at least 30 feet, between them to lessen the attraction.

Or maybe your horse wants to head back to the barn. Whatever her desires, she's got to listen to you. Give her the aids more insistently. Use your progression of aids.

What to do if . . . the horse won't follow the path of the circle.

Outside influences, such as other horses or the barn, could be distracting her, or you could be making technical errors in your aids. Ask your instructor.

Inside or Outside?

In the world of riding, we never say "left leg" or "right leg." It gets too confusing when you're switching directions. Instead, we say the "inside" or the "outside" leg.

The inside leg is always the leg on the inside of the circle you're working. The outside leg is always the leg on the outside of the circle. If you're riding to the left, or counterclockwise, your left leg is the inside leg, and your right leg is the outside leg.

This inside/outside leg stuff doesn't matter much when you go straight. But you can't keep going straight forever — there's always a beltway or an ocean to force you into making a turn.

Dismounting

You're most vulnerable to injury when dismounting and mounting, because if the horse moves, you're not securely in the saddle. To reduce your vulnerability while dismounting, avoid having one foot in the stirrup, just in case the horse moves. That's why the following dismounting method is the safest:

Dismounting a Horse

1. Gather both reins and some mane in your left hand.
2. Take *both* feet out of the stirrups **(a)**.
3. With both hands on the front of the saddle (the **pommel**), start to swing your right leg back and over the cantle. As your right leg comes over your horse's rump, take the weight into both arms.
4. After your right leg comes over, it should meet the left leg, and you should land gently on your toes, with your knees flexed **(b)**.

You're on track if you can:

✓ Comfortably lead a horse from barn to ring.
✓ Gracefully mount (well, let's just say if you can get on the horse).
✓ Keep your horse away from other horses.
✓ Walk in a straight line with a reasonably correct riding position.
✓ Implement the progression of the aids.
✓ Turn the horse to the left and right.
✓ Turn a complete circle.
✓ Halt.
✓ Dismount.
✓ Laugh and have a great time!

Seven Rules for Keeping Safe around Horses

By nature a docile animal, the horse has no wish to harm you. He may even want to serve you, within reason. I'm going to provide some general "don'ts" to help keep you safe around horses. If you obey these instructions whenever you're around a horse, it's unlikely that you'll ever be injured.

- **Don't get stepped on.** This rule is much like the warning on your lawn mower that tells you to keep your feet from underneath. If a horse's foot comes down on your toes, you'll get hurt.

- **Don't get bitten.** To avoid getting bitten, don't come between two horses biting at each other. Don't stick your fingers into a horse's mouth. Don't carry in your pocket carrots or other tempting treats that a horse may try to find with her mouth. Don't sharply tighten the horse's girth.

  Also, stay away from other horses when you're riding or leading a horse, and always have control of your horse's head, whether the horse has on a bridle or a halter and rope.

- **Don't get butted.** If a horse butts you with her head, it's usually an accident. Although it can hurt, a butt seldom results in serious injury.

  A noise or unexpected movement can startle a horse or she may panic if her bridle or the reins become caught on something. She might also react quickly to another horse that is behaving in a threatening manner, and if you happen to be in the way, you might get butted.

- **Don't get kicked.** People worry more about getting kicked than they do about getting bitten, but few actually are kicked, especially at lesson barns with well-trained school horses. There are, however, ways to help ensure you never get kicked.

  Don't make sudden movements around a horse, and never corner one in a threatening manner. Horses generally prefer to run from danger, but if they can't, they may strike out. Always let the horse know where you are.

Although a horse can kick out in any direction, it's especially important to stay away from the rear end, where a kick can be especially powerful. If you must pass behind a horse, leave about 12 feet of clearance.

If you need to get near a horse's rear to, for example, groom her, make sure it's a horse you know is well behaved. If you don't know, ask someone who does. Always keep one hand on the horse while you groom with the other to let her know where you are. Stay close to the horse and to the side of the hindquarters; avoid standing directly a foot or two behind her, because that's where the impact would be the greatest if you were to get kicked.

- **Don't fall off.** Riders who become overconfident or too relaxed make mistakes. You can be caught off guard if the horse is startled or spooks, so be tuned in to your attitude and your actions.

- **Don't ride without a helmet.** The helmet should carry a label that says it complies with ASTM/SEI guidelines. This means that the helmet meets a standard of the American Standard for Testing Materials and that it has been approved by the Safety Equipment Institute. If you do fall off or collide with something while riding a horse, the helmet will help protect your head. It's even a good idea to wear your helmet when you're bridling, working around, or standing near a horse, just in case you accidentally get butted.

- **Don't get sloppy.** Reread these rules before every lesson and keep reading them until every single one becomes second nature. As you gain experience you'll become more confident, but even then don't ignore any of these rules. If you do, you'll get hurt.

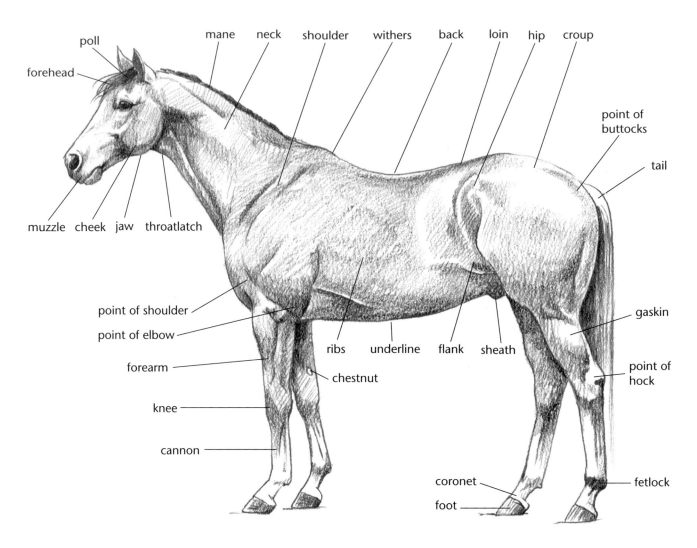

Parts of the Horse

Horses are large, solid-hoofed herbivores, which means that they eat only plants. They generally weigh anywhere from 800 to 1,400 pounds, averaging about half a ton!

Learning to Trot

IN THIS LESSON, you'll meet another school horse (or two). You'll learn more about horse personalities and handling horses. Then you'll learn how to ask the horse to trot and how to post to the trot. In order to achieve more control of the horse, you'll also learn more about applying the progression of the aids.

Your horse for today is Nemesis.

Nemesis

AGE: 7 years old
WEIGHT: 1,200 lbs.
SIZE: 17 hands (get out the ladder)

BREED: Appaloosa
COLOR: Appaloosa is a color and a breed, too!
SEX: Gelding

Very tall, sleek, and muscular, Nemesis can be wild, bossy, and a real bully in the field. He tries to keep other horses away from the hay bale if he's eating and the water trough if he's drinking.

In his stall, he doesn't much like people disturbing him, especially at dinner time. If anyone walks by, he makes ugly faces. He sticks his head over the stall door, lays back his ears, shows his teeth, and waves his head. He consistently acts up when being shown for sale, which is why he's never been sold and why you're about to ride him.

Once he's tacked up, though, Nemesis's behavior generally improves, although he's been known to issue a nip if his girth is cranked up too tight, too fast. Under saddle, he's considered frisky. He'll also act up if the rider doesn't let him know who's boss or gets too confident too soon and doesn't stay on guard.

Can you handle this horse? The instructor wouldn't have assigned him to you if she didn't think you could. Guess you'd better go tame the beast. There he stands, looking his nasty, unenthusiastic self, with his saddle and bridle on. Someone on the barn staff hands him to you.

You lead him out of his stall. He towers over you. He's not really doing anything bad, but he walks very fast, pulling you along. When you tug backwards on the reins, he stops pulling, but now he's almost trotting in place. He's snorting a lot. He tosses his head up and down. Your stomach is in a knot. Maybe you'd better tell the instructor you aren't comfortable handling Nemesis. This horse will be fun to ride after you've learned more.

Good work! You're probably going to be a great rider and a safe one, too. You're expressing what you can and cannot handle, what you are and are not comfortable doing.

Always communicate your fears, desires, and concerns to your instructor. It's possible to have a mismatch or personality conflict with a horse, and a simple request to change horses can usually be accommodated. But I've found that students too often hesitate to speak with their instructors.

It's also possible to have a personality conflict with your instructor or classmates, or to feel dissatisfied with the progress of your class. If this is the case, request a change. Students don't do this enough because they fear they'll insult their instructor, but if the instructor is a pro, one of her primary concerns will be satisfying you.

In this case, your instructor quickly reassigns you to ride a horse named Toby.

Well, this guy's a big one too. His head and feet are huge. You'd better be extra careful to keep your toes out from under his hooves. Toby is obviously very friendly. He looks happy to see you. He nuzzles you. You breathe a sign of relief. Toby leads out calmly to the ring. Don't forget to check that girth before the lesson begins.

Toby

AGE: 12
WEIGHT: 1,150 lbs.
SIZE: 15.1 hands
BREED: Draft Cross

COLOR: Bay with white
  blaze
SEX: Gelding

Toby is a Draft Cross — a cross between a *Draft* (a large horse bred to pull heavy loads) and another, smaller breed. Although of average height, he's big boned and bulky, and his feet are twice the usual size. He has a long, full black mane and tail, giving him a playful appearance, and playful he is. In the field, he's silly. He likes to take the halters off other horses with his teeth. You'll also find him rubbing his neck on trees a lot.

Especially sweet and docile with people, Toby provides a calm and steady mount. He proves that you can't judge a horse's temperament by his size. He's patient with beginners and won't do anything crazy, even if you make mistakes. But like many Draft Crosses, he has a well-deserved reputation for laziness, which can present a challenge for riders. Toby can be stubborn and refuse to go.

Introduction to the Trot

A *trot* is a two-beat gait, somewhat faster than the walk. The horse's legs move in diagonal pairs (for instance, the left front and right hind). It's important to understand how the horse moves at the trot, because each time Toby's feet hit the ground, you're going to get a shock to your derriere.

To absorb the shock, your best option is to **post** at the trot, which means rhythmically lifting out of your seat with the movement of the horse. This makes riding the horse more comfortable. The posting trot is also called *rising to the trot*.

Many riding schools begin teaching the trot only after several mounted lessons at the walk. I prefer to teach the posting trot to new riders as soon as they catch on to mounting, sitting correctly, walking, and turning. An early introduction to the trot not only gets riders moving on the horse, which they generally want to do, but also demonstrates that they need to learn a lot to ride well.

Calf Stretch

When you learn to post to the trot, you'll be using the muscles in your calves a lot more. To stretch and strengthen them, stand on a step with the balls of your feet on the edge. Grab a hand rail or balance yourself against a wall. Gently let your heels drop below the balls of your feet, hold for two seconds, lift up for two seconds, and lower for two. Repeat five times initially. Do more as you're able.

◄

When trotting, a horse places both a front foot and a hind foot on the ground with every step, making the trot a two-beat gait.

1   1   2   2

Learning the Posting Trot

If Toby wasn't used in a lesson prior to yours, your instructor probably will have you review last week's lesson as a warm-up for the horse.

After that, you're ready to begin. Start by standing up in the stirrups to improve your balance on the horse. You may find yourself wanting to grab the reins to help you up, but that makes Toby back up, so it's not a good idea.

To stand up, hold onto the mane or the front of the saddle, and stand straight up. Now you're going to sit directly down into the saddle without letting your feet move. If you stood up correctly, your lower leg is in the proper position. Your feet are under your body mass; don't let them move when you sit back down.

Try it again, but this time when you rise, lean your body forward slightly. Feel the horse with your calves. The action is more forward than up; your hips move toward your hands. Keep practicing until you can do this easily, without holding onto mane or reins. You should feel more like you're kneeling rather than sitting.

After standing up and sitting down several times without falling forward or backward, you're ready to try the trot. First, though, you have to know how to tell Toby to trot:

Aids to the Trot

1. Sit down.
2. Squeeze with your legs.
3. Push with your back.
4. Give with your hands.

Yes, these are the same aids you use when you ask the horse to walk. But you insist a bit more to encourage the horse to trot instead of walk. The farther back you position your legs and the harder you squeeze, the more aggressive are your leg aids.

You'll feel two bounces for every stride the horse takes. You'll be in the air when these bounces occur, and sitting in the saddle between them. You sit for only a fraction of a second. It's really more like touching the saddle with your butt than sitting down.

Go left around the ring. Chances are that the first time you ask Toby to trot, your derriere is going to bounce! bounce! bounce! against the seat. That's okay. You're learning.

Does this hurt Toby? It's certainly going to make him uncomfortable, and you're going to owe him an extra carrot or two after class. But hopefully you won't be doing this for long, and Toby's a patient fellow. Teaching you is how he earns his oats.

Focus on finding the rhythm of the horse. There's a definite sequence to the horse's bouncing. Learn to feel it. Pivot forward from your knees, taking your hips toward your hands and then back. Avoid moving your body straight up and down. Remember, you should feel like you're kneeling.

Keys to Learning the Posting Trot

- You should feel more like you're kneeling than sitting.

- Your hips should move forward toward your hands and then back, not so much up and down.

Learning Tips

I can't stress enough the importance of observing riders who know how to post. In my experience, students who watch other lessons or go to competitions to watch more experienced riders learn twice as fast. It motivates them. Talk to other riders. Tell them about any problems you have. They're likely to be helpful and encouraging, and you may just find a very valuable friend, but like many others, horse people won't offer advice unless asked. Except for your instructor, of course.

Posting to the trot involves subtlety and rhythm; following motion, not resisting motion.

Remember, as you post, the pivot point is your knee. Now you're beginning to move in harmony with the horse. Unless you're an engineer, forget trying to figure out the mechanics of the trot and your movements, and *feel* the trot instead.

When you first learn to post, your upper body will probably lean slightly forward. That's okay for now and actually will make it easier for you to learn. As you progress, however, your seat will become deeper because your stirrups will be longer and your thighs straighter. The tendency to lean forward will lessen or, hopefully, vanish altogether.

In time, you'll have the perfect balanced seat. In fact, you can tell how well people ride (**balance seat**) by observing how they sit at the halt on a horse. The more perpendicular their thighs are to the ground (the more their knees point downward) the better their seat. The more the angulation — that is, the more their thighs come up and their knees point forward — the shallower their seat.

A proper seat, and especially maintaining a proper seat while posting, takes time to learn. Count on at least one hour of work to get the hang of the posting trot (and I mean real sweat time), because there's a lot going on. You've got to control the horse, tell him where to go, and at the same time coordinate your movements with his. While you're learning, you're likely to encounter at least one of the following problems.

◄

When posting to the trot, your pivot point is at your knees; your feet remain in the same position.

***What to do if . . . you're bouncing around wildly and your butt smacks
the seat hard every time you come down.***

You haven't yet found the horse's rhythm. You're probably also posting
straight up and lifting yourself from your feet instead of posting
forward and back, pivoting from your knees. Chances are that your
heels are higher than your toes. Work on feeling the rhythm.

What to do if . . . you're falling forward or backward.

If your feet are too far out in front, you'll fall backward. If your feet are
too far back, you'll fall forward. Your feet must remain under your body
mass to find the correct balance.

What to do if . . . the horse goes faster.

A common mistake among beginners is riding with the reins too long
or holding onto the pommel. (Tip: You can pull on the pommel and the
horse will never slow down.) Keep your reins the proper length and
keep those hands in their proper position: just two inches above the
withers and four inches apart. If necessary, go back to the beginning of
this lesson and practice posting at the halt until you can stand independently, without supporting yourself on the horse's mane or the reins.

Another common problem is gripping with the legs, and especially
the heels. If the horse's eyes bulge or deep depressions mark the horse's
sides, you've probably had him in a death grip. Relax, and the horse
will too. It doesn't take that much contact to post.

What to do if . . . the horse keeps stopping.

Horses tend to do things at the same place at the same time. If your horse
stopped at the outgate this time, you can bet tomorrow morning's donuts
that he'll also do it the next time around. About 30 feet before you reach
the outgate, assume he's going to try it again, and aggressively encourage
him to move forward. See? You're controlling his thinking now.

Also consider that you may be pulling back on the reins to stand up.
Try to find the correct body position, because then you won't need to pull
on the reins.

About School Horses

School horses are very special creatures. They have different people riding them all
the time, many of them beginners, all using slightly different aids because they're just
learning them. It's easy for a horse to get confused under such circumstances.

Generally, if school horses get confused, they'll slow down or stop altogether.
You might think they're comatose. But this is one of the reasons they were
selected to be school horses. Other horses that get confused might do the
opposite: take off or get crazy. School horses may tend to be slower and less
responsive, but they're also tolerant and forgiving. You might get frustrated riding
them, but it's better to be frustrated than fractured. So always give school horses
the gratitude and respect they deserve.

The Crop

Suppose you're sure that you aren't pulling on the reins, that you're giving with your hands, and that your position is about as good as it can get for now, and Toby still keeps stopping. You give him the aids to move on and he takes a little step, then stops again. You give a kick with your heels, to no avail. You kick him again, harder, and get no response. You give him several hard kicks in succession and Toby still hasn't budged. Now what do you do? I warned you that Toby didn't have much of a work ethic. He's decided that class is over and he's ready to go back to his stall. If you want to finish this lesson, you're going to have to give him more encouragement, which comes in the form of a crop.

Crop is just a fancy word for a stick. In riding, it's considered an extension of the leg. In other words, when your leg doesn't work, you might use a crop. But you never use a crop without first trying your leg. A crop is a crutch, and hopefully in a few lessons you won't need one because you'll have learned to use your legs more effectively. In the meantime, just carrying a stick will encourage many horses to respond.

You hold the crop in the palm of your hand on the side that needs additional support. For most school horses, this is the inside hand because they often drift in. It can be a bit awkward carrying a crop while holding the reins, but you'll soon get used to it.

Never assume you should carry a crop. Only carry one if the instructor gives it to you. Never pass a crop to another mounted rider; you could cause either horse to shy. And certainly never, ever, loop the handle of the crop around your wrist; you may need to drop the crop quickly.

If your horse unexpectedly speeds up or does anything you don't like or find odd, drop the crop *immediately*. If the horse began going faster when you were trying to halt, you probably pulled back on the reins, which raised your hands. That brought the crop up and into the horse's sight, which he interpreted as a threatening gesture, causing him to go faster. Drop the crop. But don't throw it! Let it slide out of your hand quietly onto the ground. Crops are inexpensive, so don't worry about losing them.

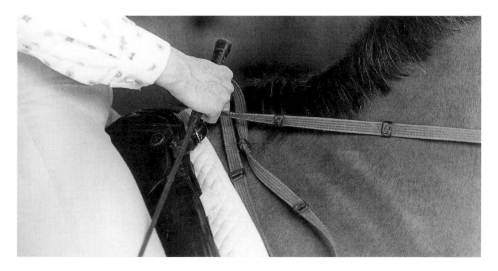

◄

The crop lies in the palm of your hand, held in place by your thumb, forefinger, and pinky.

Now try trotting again. Toby seems to have gotten the message and he's moving along nicely. Make one full lap around the ring. Get used to the rhythm. Stopping and starting a lot won't help. Try to keep him trotting at the same pace. Don't forget to steer. Try to post to the rhythm of the horse.

If you're still having trouble figuring when to post forward and when to sit, narrow your focus. Concentrate exclusively on your forward hip motion. Try to keep Toby's speed constant so his rhythm also stays constant. Avoid sharp turns, which makes it harder for the horse to maintain his pace.

A Faster or Slower Trot

Now that you've got your horse moving, try speeding him up (adding impulsion) with the correct aids. Relax pressure on the reins a bit and close both legs simultaneously. By closing your legs, I don't mean you should steadily squeeze. Instead, pulse with your upper calves in time with the horse's stride or your post. Add a driving motion to your legs. Go halfway around the ring at the faster trot, and then ask him to return to a slower trot.

To slow down the trot, increase the pressure on the reins while decreasing the pressure from your legs. If the horse comes to a stop, you issued your aids too strongly. Try again. Trot him out, establish a faster trot, and this time give the aids more gently. Slowing him down requires a fine balance between your legs and hands.

How Long Do Horses Live?

Contrary to popular belief, horses are not done for by the time they reach 10. Thanks to improved health care, many horses live well into their 20s, and some into their 30s. Some ponies live to be 40 or more. The older they are, the more they know. Some school horses have equine Ph.D.s.

Coordinating Hand and Leg Aids

When learning to trot, coordinating hand and leg aids becomes imperative. This is referred to as having the horse "between your legs and hands." If you let up the pressure on the reins, the horse should immediately speed up a bit. If you reduce the pressure from your legs, the horse should immediately slow down a bit.

Here's my point: You cannot use a hand aid without a corresponding leg aid, and you can never use a leg without using your back. For every step the horse takes, you tell him when and how fast. You do this through subtle shifts in position and the intensity of the pressure from your hands, legs, and back.

When a horse doesn't obey, we usually call it an evasion, which you'll learn more about in lesson 6. But keep in mind that a horse's apparent disobedience may not be his fault. If the instructor can mount the horse and get him to do what you were unable to, that tells you the problem lies in how you're riding. That's okay, because you're learning. But don't mistakenly blame the horse.

Learning aids is like learning a new, complex language. It requires you to communicate using body movements, which can frustrate both you and the horse.

Look at it this way. Say your phone rings and you answer, but the person on the other end is speaking a foreign language you can't understand. Eventually, you hang up. That's exactly what your horse will do to you if he can't understand. To communicate, you have to speak the same language. The horse certainly can't learn yours, so you've got to learn his.

There's one more intangible in controlling a horse: a combination of determination, confidence, respect, and compassion. We see it from time to time in our everyday lives. When people with these characteristics walk into a room, everybody notices them because they have a certain posture, an aura — what we call presence. The best riders have the same qualities.

Horses Are Not Statues

Some beginning riders needlessly worry if their horses don't stand completely still at the halt. Don't. This is normal behavior.

If asked to stand still for more than a few minutes, a horse will shift his weight from leg to leg. He's just getting comfortable. If he hasn't been adequately sprayed with insect repellent and the flies and gnats are bad, he'll twitch his muscles, swish his tail, shake his head occasionally, or even stomp his feet.

If your horse fidgets and you aren't sure if the behavior is normal and non-threatening, don't hesitate to ask your instructor.

Posting to the Diagonal

If you watch more advanced riders, you'll notice that when riding around a ring they always rise to the trot when a particular pair of the horse's legs moves forward. When the horse's outside shoulder moves forward, they rise, and as the inside shoulder moves forward, they sit.

A lot of instructors focus on teaching *diagonals*. That's because anyone who will eventually participate in horse shows needs to know how to ride to the correct diagonal. And at higher levels of riding, which include intricate circle patterns, riding on the correct diagonal not only increases your comfort, but also is important to the balance of the horse.

However, I think instructors spend too much time teaching diagonals. Most beginning students have to look down to match their post to the outside shoulder when they should instead pay attention to where they're going. So why am I even mentioning diagonals? At some point, your instructor probably will want you to learn them.

Master the posting trot before you attempt to post to the correct diagonal. Ideally, you'll be able to feel when the horse's outside shoulder moves forward and you won't have to look down. Unfortunately, it's unlikely you'll be able to do that soon. So when you do look down, try to make it a quick glance — just the second or two it takes for you to see the outside shoulder move. If you discover you're on the incorrect diagonal, simply sit down for an odd number of bounces, which will put you on the correct diagonal.

Once you're in tune with your horse and posting on the correct diagonal, don't look down again, unless you accidentally sit an extra bounce or the horse missteps and throws off your rhythm. If that happens, once again glance down just enough to catch that forward outside shoulder motion, and then refocus on where you're going. Otherwise, you might never get there.

▶
To post to the correct diagonal, rise out of your seat when the horse's outside shoulder moves forward.

You're on track if you can:

✓ Trot your horse at a slow and a slightly faster speed.

✓ Post to the trot.

✓ Use a crop safely.

✓ Coordinate your hand and leg aids more frequently.

Warning Signs

The safety section in lesson 1 focused on your behavior around horses. But to stay safe, you also need to recognize when a horse shows warning signs of impending trouble.

a

- **His ears are laid back on his head (a).** This could be described as making an ugly face. It's definitely not pretty. The horse looks fierce, and he means to. If you're leading a horse and he lays back his ears and makes a face, calmly call to an instructor or some other nearby experienced person for help.

  In the meantime, keep control of the horse's head by holding the reins or lead rope about five or six inches away from the horse's mouth; if the horse moves, a strong check is in order. Be sure to stand at the horse's shoulder, not in front of him.

- **His tail swishes.** Horses swish their tails to get rid of flies, but sharp, rapid swishes also can signal irritation. You need to learn the difference. A horse grazing in a pasture on a hot summer day is most likely trying to get rid of flies by swishing. If a mounted horse starts swishing his tail because the horse and rider behind him are too close, look out. Chances are he's irritated.

  You're more likely to notice this problem if you're the one on the second horse. Stay at least one horse length away from the horse in front to avoid a possible kick.

  If you're on the ground, remember never to walk up behind a horse, especially one that's swishing his tail.

b

- **His eyes widen and the white around the iris shows.** This usually indicates that the horse has been surprised, is in distress, or is frightened. Calmly but immediately call out to the instructor.

- **His nostrils are flared and he's fidgeting and sweating (b).** This indicates a very upset, nervous horse. Ask for another horse or ask your instructor to ride the horse first to confirm that he's calm enough for you to use in your lesson.

- **He turns his rump to you.** This usually occurs in the stall. The horse doesn't want you to approach him. Get someone with more experience to handle him.

Lesson 3

Riding in a Field

THIS LESSON IS ONE OF THE MOST ENJOYABLE you'll have. Riding in a field without the ring around you and with no locked gate gives you a wonderful sense of freedom and a glimmer of what's farther down the road in your riding career. In fact, riding in a field can be downright exhilarating.

In this lesson you'll not only get a chance to see how well you've mastered the basic skills of walking, trotting, turning, and stopping, you're going to learn a lot more about the importance of outside influences on the horse.

You're learning by now that, just as people differ, so do horses. Some are friendly, some aren't; some don't mind working, and others do. Each horse requires an individual approach. Today, you'll need to learn to manage Tiki.

Tiki

AGE: 14
WEIGHT: 1,100 lbs.
SIZE: 15.3 hands
BREED: Thoroughbred

COLOR: Dark bay with white blaze, stockings, and socks
SEX: Gelding

Although strikingly beautiful, with a shiny coat and sleek build, Tiki has an ugly disposition. He just isn't friendly. He sulks in the back of his stall much of the time and glares at anyone who comes near. If you give him a treat, he acts like he's doing you a favor by taking it. He's a sophisticated, grumpy old man, but all bluff and no bite.

Other horses regard him as a bit of a misfit. In the field, he gets picked on by pint-sized ponies. He's basically considered a wimp.

Despite his less-than-charming nature, Tiki has never harmed a human being. He's just come to associate people with something he doesn't want to do, namely, work. With his posture, he's telling you to go away. But under saddle, he's spirited and knowledgeable. Compared to other school horses, he's advanced. In addition to being responsive, he moves forward willingly, but not dangerously so. He has impulsion. You won't need a crop.

Approaching and handling a horse like Tiki requires thought and skill. When you enter his stall, he may be standing in the back, sulking as usual. Approach him from the side, the least threatening direction, and keep your arms down.

Calmly, slowly, and confidently, touch his neck or shoulder first. Do not try to pet him on the head first, which many people do. Many of us are naturally drawn to the horse's beautiful eyes, but many horses don't like their faces touched. They've gotten one too many fingers in their eyes.

When you encounter a less-than-cooperative horse like Tiki, never let him get between you and the door, and never close and lock the stall door behind you. You want to be able to exit quickly, if necessary. And remember, if Tiki or any other horse turns his butt toward you, lays back his ears, bares his teeth, or swishes his tail at you, don't enter the stall. If you're already in the stall, leave. Self-protection comes first. Then ask your instructor what to do. Good instructors really don't mind your asking for help; they welcome the opportunity to teach, and this is the kind of situation that can provide an important learning opportunity.

You'll find that with horses, especially those like Tiki, your body posture says a lot. Tiki can intimidate people, but if he hasn't issued any aggressive warning signs, you can handle Tiki yourself.

In you go. Confident, calm. You approach him from the side and pat him on the shoulder. He gives you a dirty look, but that's all. You take the reins off his neck and over his head, and lead him out. You walk him to the ring for mounting.

Outside Influences

Think about this: Without the ring around the horse to contain him, the draw of the barn will be greater than ever. Horses associate the barn with food, and eating is what they like to do most. They also don't have to work when in their stalls, so that's where they want to be.

Horses in a field are more gregarious. They sense greater freedom without the constraints of the ring. This makes outside influences even more problematic. Tiki will feel friskier.

Horses are competitive. If a horse is following several others, he'll go faster to get to the front. If the horse in front senses a horse moving up, he'll go faster. This isn't much of a problem if you're riding in second or third place, but if you're fifth or sixth in line, look out. A chain reaction can begin.

Modified Leg Lunge

Here's another leg-strengthening exercise.

Stand with your feet about shoulder width apart. Take one step forward with your right foot. Bend both knees until the left knee is about one foot off the floor, then slowly rise and bring the left leg forward. When bending, keep your knee even with or behind the toes of the forward foot. Repeat the exercise with your left foot forward. Do three repetitions on each leg at first and gradually build up.

An open area will also heighten the horse's sense of self-preservation. Good school horses generally don't spook, especially near the barn, but there's always a Dixie around: a big, beautiful horse that panics at her own shadow and regards little rabbits as horse-eaters. For some horses, a cricket that jumps and hits the belly is enough to cause a scare. In other cases, horses aren't really scared of varmints in the field, but if they see one, they'll use it as an excuse to act up.

The horse's main line of defense is to flee. When in doubt about his safety, he'll run away first, often toward the barn, and think about it later. And if one horse runs, the others will want to follow.

For the rider, the challenge is to override these outside influences. You need to be twice as alert and vigilant about controlling your horse's thoughts. You need to reassure him that he's in a safe environment. How do you do this? By communicating using your weight, your hands, and your legs. This keeps his focus on *you*. Remember this as you go through this lesson.

▲
When riding outside the ring, make sure you maintain a safe distance apart.

Ask Questions

Get your money's worth out of your lessons and speed up your progress: Ask your instructor questions! Don't try to figure it all out yourself. Your instructor can quckly help you resolve a problem that otherwise might take you hours to answer. By asking questions, you initiate a response that benefits both you and the instructor. It also can make riding more fun and safer too.

Don't worry about sounding stupid. For beginning riders, there are no stupid questions. If you're in a group lesson, other students are probably having the same problem.

When you do finally grasp a skill that frustrated you, go ahead and make a big deal of it. Let everyone share in your success. Doing so encourages other students and adds to the fun.

◄

A good instructor welcomes questions and does her best to prepare students for what they'll encounter in the field.

Mounting Outside the Ring

At this stage your instructor probably will continue to have you mount in the ring, and rightfully so. After all, you haven't ridden a horse outside the ring yet and haven't faced all those outside influences.

When the time comes for you to mount outside the ring, however, remember that you won't have nice, soft ring dirt underneath you. In a field, select the softest spot or the place least likely to cause damage if you hit the ground. Avoid rocky areas (or, for that matter, gravel driveways and parking lots). Remember, mounting and dismounting leave you the most vulnerable to injury.

Here are some other tips for mounting outside of a ring:

- Point your horse away from the barn. This will reduce the pull of the barn. Your horse will be more likely to stand still while you mount him.
- Always mount on the uphill side. Why make a horse taller and harder to mount than he already is?
- Keep your horse's head up. A field is likely to have grass, which he will want to eat.
- Check the girth!

Time to Enjoy

Budget plenty of time for your lessons. Arrive early and watch the more advanced students ride. If you're taking group lessons, get to know your classmates. Ask an instructor if you can help groom a horse, but explain that you're a novice and will need supervision and instruction. You can learn a lot just by hanging around. Learn, relax, and enjoy the barn atmosphere.

This may be the best advice I've given you yet.

Controlling the Horse

Now you're mounted and ready to walk out the gate and line up for a ride in the field, around the outside of the ring. Begin walking Tiki in an orderly fashion; all horses should be safely spaced one horse length apart.

Tiki's definitely different from other horses you've ridden. You just barely gave the aids to the walk and he moved forward. Compared to the others, Tiki feels downright energetic. You know already that you won't need to use your aids as aggressively as you did with Toby in lesson 2. But be alert. This guy could move out fast if he wants to.

After walking around the outside of the ring, you're ready to pick up a posting trot. Pretty soon, you'll be riding the open range. But oops! A few things go wrong, and on such a perfect day.

What to do if . . . your horse slows down.

You're probably trotting away from the barn. Gently give the aids to move on. Keep him focused on you.

What to do if . . . your horse trots faster.

Now you're probably riding toward the barn, the greatest of outside influences. Or maybe your horse is feeling a bit competitive and wants to catch the horse in front of you. Don't let his mind wander, and don't let him take one step you didn't tell him to take. Issue half halts — half of a halt — as necessary. (See more on this below). If you don't, you could end up sitting on him in his stall.

The second a horse changes his pace when you didn't ask him to, correct him. If you don't, he'll keep speeding up. A horse that gets out of control is like a snowball rolling down a hill; it starts slow but picks up momentum as it rolls. I use this snowball analogy throughout the book because it brings home the point that you must anticipate the problem and fix it before it becomes dangerous.

Also check to see if the horse behind you is getting too close. Your horse won't want to let another pass him. You assume your companions know etiquette and the rules of riding. This situation requires you to put twice as much effort into controlling your own horse; you still shouldn't let him trot faster than you want.

What to do if . . . the horse is playing catch-up with the horse in front.

If you let your horse drift too far behind the others — more than three or four horse lengths — he may periodically try to catch up to them. Reduce the pull of this outside influence by keeping him properly spaced. Ride about one horse length behind the horse in front of you unless your instructor tells you otherwise.

Etiquette requires you to keep proper spacing; if you change speeds, your classmates behind you will have to do likewise. You don't want to create an accordion effect.

What to do if . . . your horse tries to get out of line.

In the ring during a class, school horses tend to cut corners and drift into the middle. They know that's where they usually get a rest while the instructor talks, so that's where they want to go. But now that you're outside the ring, your horse probably is trying to drift toward the barn. Turn him back into line. Don't let him get away with this behavior. It could be dangerous.

Beware If Your Horse Changes Pace

At this stage of riding, one of the most important points to remember is that a change of pace, whether it's slower or faster, means something. If the horse changes pace and you didn't ask him to, correct him. Remember, the horse is thinking all the time. Keep him thinking with you, not against you.

The Half Halt

The ***half halt*** is, just as the name implies, half of a halt. It's a very important way of controlling your horse. In lesson 6 you'll use this move to signal a pending change in movement to the horse. But for now, you simply want to slow Tiki down, not stop him. Start by reviewing the aids to the halt:

Aids to the Halt

1. Sit down (or stop following the horse with your back).
2. Set your hands (don't give to the horse with the reins).
3. Gently close your legs on the horse.
4. Stiffen your back, pushing into your hands.
   To make this a half halt, do these things with less intensity than you would if you were asking Tiki to halt.

Too much to remember? Then pull back on the reins just a bit. A half halt should only take a fraction of a second to accomplish. Half halt, release. Half halt again if needed, then release. Steady pulls on a horse won't work. You'll just get into a pulling match and Tiki will win.

If you issue a half halt and Tiki stops, you issued the aids too intensely. Ask Tiki to move forward and try your half halt again. The second Tiki responds, stop issuing these aids. Any time Tiki speeds up when you don't want him to, half halt him.

The World Is Not Flat

Unlike the ring, the field has uneven terrain. Try posting to the trot up a slight hill. Pretty comfortable, isn't it? That's because a horse normally carries two-thirds of his weight in the front end. When a horse goes uphill, he's more balanced because of the way gravity affects him on a hill: his weight gets distributed over all four feet.

Now try posting to the trot down a very slight hill. Not so easy or comfortable, right? That's because your horse can't shift his weight for balance on the downhill. This also makes it much harder to keep your proper riding position.

▶

The posting trot is more comfortable going uphill because the horse's weight is more evenly distributed.

▶

It is more difficult for riders to keep their balance going downhill. You must work harder to maintain your proper position.

Eventually, you'll learn how to help the horse balance himself, which will make riding over uneven terrain easier for both of you. For now, I want this experience to teach you that the horse's posture really does make a difference. Are you getting the hang of this? It's fun, isn't it?

What to do if . . . your horse won't follow the path you want.

This is probably the pull of outside influences again, most likely the barn or the other horses. When a horse does something, it's for a reason. Figure out the reason and you can correct the problem.

There could be another simple explanation: You may not be looking where you're going. Riding in a field, it's easy to become distracted. But you're on a horse! Pay attention, focus on where you are going and on communicating with your horse. If you don't, he'll decide for you what you're going to do, and you might not like his choices.

What to do if . . . *your horse suddenly feels too energetic and you're feeling unsure of yourself.*

There's a good chance that when riding in the field, your horse feels friskier than he does in the ring. Another possibility is that something really is bothering him. Maybe those crickets make him nervous. Maybe he spotted one of those killer rabbits in the bushes.

If you are riding in a field and you feel at any time that your horse is about to get out of control, immediately turn your horse away from where you were going and away from what's making him disobedient.

If possible, turn the horse toward your instructor. Let the instructor know immediately that you feel something's about to go wrong so she can help you.

Next, you have to do something that, believe it or not, is difficult. You have to *listen very carefully to your instructor.* When you get nervous, it's hard to focus, but focus you must. If you don't, things could get out of control. Force yourself to focus on what your instructor says, and do what she tells you.

You're on track if you can:

✓ Keep your horse in line while riding around the outside of the ring.
✓ Keep your horse properly spaced from other horses while riding around the outside of the ring.
✓ Keep your horse moving at a steady pace while riding around the outside of the ring.
✓ Trot up and down slight hills in a field.

Dressing for Riding

For the beginning rider, jeans will do just fine. Wear a pair without prominent seams down the inside of the legs; they can rub. Don't select jeans that are so tight that you have to lie down on the bed to squeeze into them.

In case you haven't heard, polyester pants are out. In fact, they've always been out for riding; the material is so slick that you might slide right out of the saddle.

Wear boots that will protect your feet. No sandals! Believe it or not, I've had quite a number of people over the years show up for a riding lesson with their toes exposed. Not smart. Wear a pair of hiking boots, construction boots, or some other heeled boots that will protect your feet and keep your foot from slipping through the stirrup. For beginning English riding, however, leave your cowboy boots home; they have an arch that raises your heel, incorrectly positioning it higher than your toes.

Lesson 4

The Sitting Trot

YOU LEARNED THAT THE POSTING TROT makes traveling from point **A** to point **B** more comfortable on a horse. But posting also has a downside: Because you're up and out of the saddle more than half the time, you lose a bit of control. The posting trot certainly has its place, but it falls short in these instances:

- When the horse is misbehaving
- When you're training a horse
- When the footing is rough

These are all times when you need more control over your horse and your position. To achieve that control, you need to learn to sit to the trot, instead of post. Sitting to the trot simply means that you stay in the saddle as the horse trots, which lets you exert more pressure on the horse with your weight. Eventually, you'll find the sitting trot even more comfortable than the posting trot.

Those of you who also want to learn how to ride Western certainly will want to learn to sit to the trot. Western riders seldom post to the trot, or the *jog*, as they call it.

The horse you'll ride today is Foxy.

Foxy

SIZE: 15 hands

AGE: 18   BREED: Appaloosa
WEIGHT: 950 lbs.   SEX: Gelding

Foxy is the boss among the geldings, command-ing their respect by his stoic presence.

Foxy likes to eat more than anything else in the world. He even likes his **worming paste**. He has a knack for opening stall doors, a trick he's mastered so he can get to the grain in the feed bin. Consequently, he has a double lock on his door to prevent him from gorging himself and coming down with a case of **colic**.

Despite his tough manner in the field, he's actually calm and cooperative with riders. His only drawback is that, well, he's a bit bumpy. In fact, he's been called the horse with square wheels. He teaches beginners to sit to the trot in a hurry, or wish they had.

His attitude seems to be, "Well, I may not be happy about it, but it's time to go to work." Foxy walks nicely out of his stall and to the ring. He stands quietly while you mount.

Introduction to the Sitting Trot

The aids to the sitting trot are the same aids that you learned for the trot in lesson 2, but your body moves differently as the horse moves. When the horse trots, his left front and right hind legs (and right front and left hind legs) hit the ground at the same time. His motion is not straight up and down, so yours shouldn't be either. There's a pitch and roll to it, like a ship on the high seas.

To continue with the nautical analogy, many good sailors have a peculiar posture; they tend to stand with their knees slightly flexed, which gives them a bow-legged appearance. That's because they've learned to follow the ship's motion — its pitch and roll — with their bodies, which requires angulation of the joints. By flexing their knees, they absorb shock. If their posture remained stiff and ungiving, they'd take the full brunt of the waves.

Riders must learn to give similarly. If you go with the horse's motion, you lessen the shock. If you resist it, you're in trouble. Moving in harmony with the horse is what makes the sitting trot a beautiful way to ride. If you can learn to do the sitting trot, you'll look darn good up there. Don't believe me? Watch more advanced riders. They almost exclusively sit to the trot.

Before continuing, review the aids to the trot:

Aids to the Trot

1. Sit down.
2. Squeeze with your legs.
3. Push with your back.
4. Give with your hands.

Gripping Is a Sin!

You're mounted in the ring, warmed up, and ready to go. You ask Foxy to trot and he nicely sets off down the side of the ring. You don't post. Whoa! You're bouncing straight up in the air. Your hands fly around uncontrollably. Foxy begins to speed up. Time to halt and talk about this, assuming you haven't bitten off your tongue.

Some riders pick up the sitting trot right away. If you don't, don't worry. Many students find this seat a challenge. You've actually sat to the trot already, before you learned to post. It may only have been for a few strides, but you did it.

Back and Abdominals Strengthener

Your back and abdominal muscles need to work in tandem and they need to be strong. Here's an exercise that uses both sets of muscles.

Lie down on your back. Straighten one leg and bend the other at the knee. With elbows bent, put your hands behind your head and rest your fingers gently there. (Don't pull up on your head.)

Tilt your pelvis so your lower back stays on the floor. Simultaneously lift your straight leg about eight inches and your upper body a few inches off the floor. Keep your elbows back, out of your peripheral vision, and your chin off your chest. Lower your upper body and foot to the floor simultaneously, lift up again, and then lie back. Repeat for the other leg.

This is a difficult type of sit-up, so only do a few repetitions the first time. Don't do it at all if it causes you pain anywhere. Gradually build up your stamina for this exercise.

You'll remember that I advised you not to try to analyze the mechanics of the posting trot and to try to feel it instead. With the sitting trot, however, an understanding of the mechanics can help.

The sitting trot requires balance, suppleness, and poise. Here's the bottom line, folks: If you grip, there is no way you can hold yourself in the saddle when the horse trots. You must not grip. Gripping is bad.

Remember something called surface tension from high school physics? If you let the air out of a basketball, it won't bounce because you've released the surface tension. Something having surface tension will bounce. If you grip with your legs on a saddle, you create surface tension in your buttocks and thighs, and you'll bounce. The only way to release the surface tension is to relax the grip. *Don't grip.*

Riding well also requires good balance, and for something to be well balanced, it has to have a firm base. In riding, you want to keep your base —

A Mounted Exercise to Find Your Seat Bones

This mounted exercise will take us to the next step in learning the sitting trot. Foxy is standing cooperatively at the halt. Now find your seat bones.

1. Take your feet out of the stirrups (**a**).
2. With your legs extending straight down, lift them out to the side two or three times. You should feel two definite bones in your rump. These are the lower ends of your hip bones (**b**).
3. Roll back on those seat bones. Your hips will also roll backwards. Now roll forward onto those bones. Your hips roll forward, too. Do this without moving your shoulders, raising your legs, or tightening your thighs or knees (**c**).
4. Roll back and forth quickly several times, maintaining your upper body position.

That's the sitting trot!

a   b   c

your center of gravity — as low as possible. (Men have a bit of a disadvantage here because they tend to have more muscle mass, or weight, in their top half than do women.) To keep your center of gravity low, all your weight should be directed downward, into the saddle.

To repeat, gripping raises you out of the saddle and destroys your balance. Without balance, you grip harder. Then you come up farther. Before you know it, you're bouncing wildly, the horse goes faster, and you lose control.

Remember what riding is all about. It's nothing more than balance, poise, and suppleness. Judicious contact between rider and horse preserves balance. The key word here is *judicious*.

Following the Horse

Now you're ready for Foxy to trot. Think about what you're going to do: Roll forward on your seat bones as Foxy's legs hit the ground and the shock occurs; roll back in preparation for the next shock, and then roll forward again. Rolling forward on your seat bones allows you to absorb shock. No gripping!

Here you go. Sit in your proper position, with legs gently against Foxy. Ask him to trot. Roll forward with the shock, then back. Note that the backward movement lasts just a fraction of a second. Forward with the shock (and back). Forward with the shock.

What to do if . . . you can't maintain the sitting trot.

Beginning students often sit to the trot successfully the first few strides, only to then have their position rapidly deteriorate. If this happens to you, it means you're losing your balance.

It also probably means you're gripping. As soon as you start to lose your balance, stop the horse. Come to a full halt, get a handle on the situation (notice I didn't say "get a grip"), and begin again.

What to do if . . . the horse keeps speeding up.

Your heels probably are up instead of down, and that's a sign of gripping. New riders instinctively grip to help them stay in the saddle, but it doesn't work, particularly in the sitting trot. Remember, gripping makes the horse go faster, which will make you bounce more, which will make you grip more, and so on, until you reach a full gallop. I *have* seen beginning riders fall off. Don't grip!

If you're bouncing, the horse may be going faster to escape the discomfort. Try the sitting trot for only a few strides at a time — not more than 10 — until you catch on. I promise it will be easier on both of you.

What to do if . . . your crotch is taking a beating.

You may be staying forward too long as you try to follow the horse's motion. Your heels also may be up, causing you to fall forward a bit and lose your balance. Stop and start over, thinking about keeping your proper position and a low center of gravity. Most importantly, work on following the horse's motion.

What to do if . . . you sway laterally.

If you seem to be uncontrollably shifting from left to right in the saddle, it could be that your legs are coming off the horse. Here again, focus on maintaining the proper position and a low center of gravity.

Try to relax your lower back. A stiff back may hinder you from following the roll of the horse's motion with your hips, causing your lateral shift.

What to do if . . . your hands bounce high above the withers.

This is the most common criticism instructors have for students learning the sitting trot. It takes time to learn to control your back and legs while steering the horse at the same time. When you learn to control your seat, your hands will follow. In the meantime, try to keep your arms and hands close to your body.

▶

When sitting to the trot, keep your arms and hands close to your body.

Taking It Slow

At this stage, try to sit to the trot only at a very slow speed. To ride in balance requires good control of the horse. You certainly couldn't walk a jerking tightrope after four lessons. It's the same with the horse. So take it slow.

Before you go faster, you also must learn to control the horse better by doing something called **collection**. That means asking the horse to round up his body to absorb more of the shock and provide a smoother gait. You'll learn about collection in lesson 6. For now, keep Foxy trotting at a nice, slow pace. Remember, hips forward with the shock (and back).

Relax!

The sitting trot is an elusive seat. If you try too hard when learning it, the more elusive it becomes. Your mind just can't fire your muscles fast enough. It requires a relaxed state.

You now know all the pitfalls of learning the sitting trot, so expect them. Don't get uptight when they occur. Leave those tensions and worries at home. Keep in mind that the sitting trot simply involves following the horse's motion. With practice, it will become as natural as the sailor's bending his knees to absorb the shock of the waves. I guarantee that the first time you experience it, you'll grin from sea to sea.

Don't Do It Backward

Many students think they've learned the sitting trot correctly, but they've actually learned it backward. They roll *back* with shock, instead of *forward*. Initially, with the horse going slow, this will feel comfortable. But once the horse starts to move faster, you'll bounce straight up in the air again. Why? If you sit to the trot this way, the saddle moves before you do, and you find yourself constantly playing catch-up. Your legs creep forward and your back hunches. Before you know it, the bouncing is bruising your butt and jarring your teeth. You may very likely come right out of the saddle.

So if your instructor tells you, "You're legs are too far forward and you're hunching your back," you're probably sitting to the trot backwards. This can be hard to see, even for your instructor. Make sure you roll your hips and those butt bones forward with the shock.

Private or Group Lessons?

I generally favor group lessons because students find them to be more fun. You get to meet other aspiring riders, make new friends, and share your triumphs and woes. In addition, learning to ride takes time in the saddle, and you can get in twice as much riding time in a group lesson for less cost. Group lessons usually run one hour and cost from around $20 to $25, depending on where you live; private lessons generally last half an hour and cost from $35 to $40.

If, however, you run into trouble learning a particular skill, consider taking a private lesson. Sometimes that extra instruction, combined with more practice, is all you need to get back on track.

You're on track if you can:

✓ Stay on the horse at the sitting trot (extra kudos if you don't grip or bounce).

✓ Use your arms and legs to communicate with the horse while sitting to the trot.

✓ Turn the horse while maintaining your posture.

✓ Realize when you've lost your rhythm, stop, and start over.

Why You Can't Sneak Up on a Horse

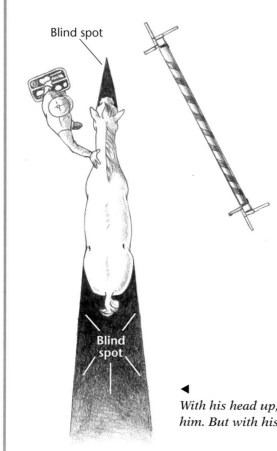

Blind spot

Blind spot

The horse's eyes have three lids. You can see two of them; the third, least visible one helps keep the eye free of dirt and dust. After all, it would be pretty difficult for the horse to wipe a speck of dust out of his eye with a 15-pound hoof, especially one that has a steel shoe on it.

Notice that the horse's eyes are located on the side of the head. That's why he can't see you well if you stand directly in front of him. He can, however, see very well to the side and, with his head down, almost in a full circle, an evolutionary adaptation that helped protect him from predators in the wild.

Even at night, you can't sneak up on a horse because his large pupils permit excellent night vision. If you're out on the trail after the sun goes down, you might need to worry about hitting your head on a branch, but you don't need to worry about the horse hitting his.

◄

With his head up, a horse can't see directly in front of him or directly behind him. But with his head down, he can see almost in a full circle.

THE
FINER
POINTS

PART 2

Lesson 5
Improving Control

THE KEY TO IMPROVING CONTROL is good communication with your horse. He's already allowed you to sit on him and ride him around. But beyond that, if he can't understand you, he can't do what you want. He doesn't have the ability to understand your verbal language. So you need to use a *tactile* language: the aids.

Aids require direct contact. Each can can be applied with varying intensity and in countless combinations.

Keep these important rules in mind as you review the material in this chapter:

- Never use a hand aid without a corresponding leg aid.
- Never use a leg aid without a back aid.
- Coordinate your legs, hands, and back.
- Always drive your horse forward and straight (unless you're bending).
- When you turn, your horse must bend into, and to the degree of, the turn.

It's time to meet your school horse for this lesson.

Watergate

AGE: 18
WEIGHT: 800 lbs.
SIZE: 14.3 hands

BREED: Arabian
COLOR: Gray

Many instructors consider *Arabians* too "hot," or on the fast and frisky side, for use as school horses. Watergate is unusual, however. He's especially well behaved and calm, and he knows the class routine better than most instructors. He's a star among school horses.

Although on the smallish side, in the field he's definitely a herd leader. (He's one of the horses that terrorizes Tiki.) Another horse had better not try to eat his pile of hay.

Under saddle, Watergate moves forward easily, but he demands that riders give him very clear instructions.

The Bit

You've learned the basic aids, but there's more to know before you can effectively communicate with Watergate. So don't mount up just yet.

Consider the ***bit***, the metal mouthpiece of the bridle. Most bridles used with school horses have stainless-steel bits, but some bits consist of other materials, such as copper and copper alloys. Copper makes a horse salivate, keeping the mouth moist and more sensitive.

Many people think the bit sits on the horse's teeth, but it doesn't. It sits on the ***bars***, a toothless section of jawbone, between the horse's front and back teeth, that is covered by gums and mucous membranes.

If someone says, "The horse took the bit and ran," it doesn't mean that the horse grabbed the bit in his teeth and took off. It means the horse angled his head so that he transferred the pressure of the bit off his bars and against the sides of his back teeth. The point I want to make is that to use the bit effectively, you work it on the horse's bars, not on his teeth.

In hot-blooded horses, such as Thoroughbreds, the membranes covering the bars are thinner than they are in cold-blooded horses, such as Drafts. To better visualize the horse's bars and the membranes covering it, think of your shin bone and its thin covering of skin. Shins generally are sensitive to bangs, scrapes, and blows. So are a horse's bars.

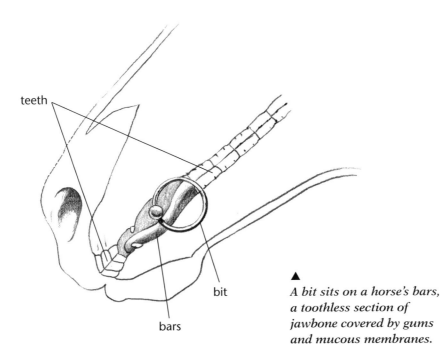

teeth

bit

bars

▲
A bit sits on a horse's bars, a toothless section of jawbone covered by gums and mucous membranes.

The Jointed Snaffle Bit

There are more bits on the market than you can count. The most common type used on school horses is called a jointed snaffle bit. It consists of two pieces of metal jointed in the middle and acts something like a nutcracker when you pull on both reins. Generally, the greater the diameter of the snaffle, the gentler it is. The thinner the snaffle, the harsher. Think of it this way: A pipe is less likely to cut you than a wire.

The snaffle connects to a cheek piece, common types being the full-cheek, the D-ring, and the ring. A full-cheek snaffle is among the mildest of bits, dispersing pressure evenly on the cheeks. A D-ring snaffle is somewhat harsher; when you tug on the right rein, the ring on the left side of the bit pulls against the horse's left cheek and into the cavity between the front and back teeth. A ring snaffle is harsher yet; it pulls into that same cavity, but it tends to be sharp sided. Ring size also affects severity: A larger ring will be less severe.

What does all this mean? Assuming you're using a rein aid that involves the cheek piece of the bit, a full-cheek snaffle requires more pressure than a ring snaffle to obtain the desired result.

Although I've used the words "severe" and "harsh," know that, in general, a snaffle bit used correctly is the gentlest of bits. Accordingly, it's less likely than other types of bits to hurt the horse if you make mistakes using it.

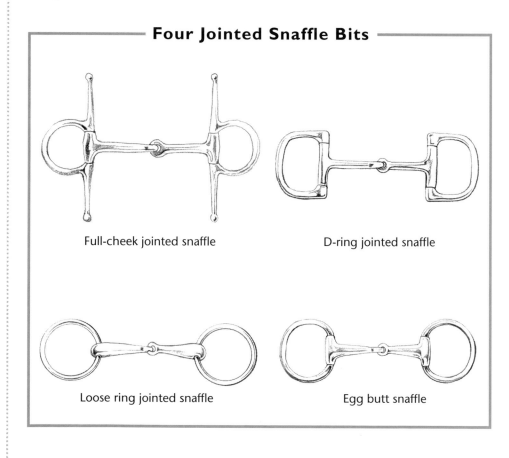

Four Jointed Snaffle Bits

Full-cheek jointed snaffle

D-ring jointed snaffle

Loose ring jointed snaffle

Egg butt snaffle

Leverage Bits

A leverage bit is far more severe than a snaffle bit. Commonly used types of leverage bits are the pelham and Kimberwick. These are used with a curb strap or chain that fits under the horse's chin. When you pull on the reins you create pressure between the mouthpiece and the curb. These bits generally give more control than a snaffle bit.

I might use a leverage bit in a very hard-mouthed horse, not because he's going to run away, but just to get him to listen. Generally, however, I don't use this type of bit on one of my school horses.

If you're riding English and are given a horse with a leverage bit, ask why, and ask how you should use it.

Pelham bit with curb chain

Rein Aids

For this lesson, you should assume that Watergate's bit is a jointed snaffle. (In fact, some of the rein aids I discuss won't even work with a leverage bit.)

Here's an important point: The severity of most rein aids is determined by the pressure in the *off* hand. Remember, a jointed snaffle acts like a nutcracker. It takes both reins to initiate the nutcracker action. If you pull on the left rein but have no tension in the right rein, minimal or no nutcracker action results. If, however, you pull on the left rein and maintain tension in the right rein, the nutcracker effect comes into play, making the aid more severe.

Now you should be ready to mount Watergate and try out the following rein aids. By this time, you're probably a pro at leading the horse out of the barn, checking the girth, and mounting. Take a minute to realize all you've learned and congratulate yourself.

I'll discuss the rein aids in ascending order of severity.

To apply a leading rein to the inside, move your inside hand out to the side.

To apply a direct rein, close your inside hand and give a corresponding amount with your outside hand.

Leading Rein

While trotting on right rein around the ring — with your right hand on the inside of the circle — move your inside right hand out to the side to tell the horse to turn. It's not a sharp turn, but Watergate turns.

You've just applied a leading rein. Intended for general training and riding when fine control of the horse isn't a major consideration, it's the only single-action rein aid you can use. A single-action rein aid is one that does not require tension in the other hand. You simply utilize the sides of the bit on the horse's cheeks without closing the nutcracker. In essence, you lead him in the direction that you want to go.

Direct Rein

Now you want to ask Watergate to make a sharper turn than before. Get him trotting again. Close your inside hand (that is, pull gently on the rein) and give a corresponding amount with the outside hand, which should still maintain tension.

You've just used a mild direct rein. Was Watergate's turn sharper than the preceding one? If so, you used the aid correctly. What determines the severity is not how much you pull on one rein, but the tension in the outside rein.

The direct rein tends to make the horse bend his body into the turn. By increasing the bend, you'll get a sharper, crisper turn than you would by using a leading rein.

Now try a harsher version of the direct rein. Instead of merely closing your inside hand, pull it toward your inside hip, and totally resist that action with the other hand. The nutcracker is closing and Watergate should turn even more sharply. However, don't forget that you should never use your hand without a leg. Generally, if the rein aid is harsher, the leg aid will have to be proportionally more aggressive. Otherwise, the horse will slow down or stop.

The harsher the direct rein aid, the crisper the turn. If Watergate moves in a very small circle, you've issued a harsh direct rein aid. Again, when I say "harsh," I do not mean to imply that you are hurting Watergate. You are simply applying a more dramatic aid.

Indirect Rein behind the Withers

Next, you're going to try something called an indirect rein behind the withers. Note that I said *behind*, not across, the withers. You never want to bring your hand across the withers or cross the center line of the horse. Doing so bends the horse's neck too much. Anyway, it's the backward, not the sideways, movement of the rein that works.

To apply an indirect rein behind the withers, begin by moving your inside hand behind the withers, toward the opposite hip. What you do

with your other hand determines the severity of the aid and therefore the result. To make a circle, for instance, use a simple direct rein aid on the outside hand. Your turn should be even sharper and crisper than before because this rein aid closes the nutcracker tighter and exaggerates the bend of the horse.

The indirect rein behind the withers can also be combined with other outside rein aids. Say Watergate starts to cut corners as you trot him around the ring. If you use an indirect rein behind the withers on the inside and a leading rein on the outside, he will drift to the outside instead of turning in. In other words, you bend him around the corner with the inside hand while your outside hand supports him enough to keep him on the rail.

▲

An indirect rein behind the withers, applied by moving your inside hand toward your opposite hip, can be made more severe by combining it with outside rein aids.

Indirect Rein in Front of the Withers

An indirect rein in front of the withers will create the sharpest turn yet. No matter what your outside hand does, this closes the nutcracker more than the other rein aids. It's handy for negotiating a tight course of jumps or sharp turns on the trail when you're riding at a faster pace.

Begin by moving your inside hand in front of the withers, up toward the horse's opposite shoulder. It's a lifting action. For a simple turn, combine this with a direct rein on the outside.

◄

An indirect rein in front of the withers, applied by moving your inside hand in front of the withers, often is used to negotiate a tight course of jumps.

Pulley Rein

If you ever find yourself on a runaway horse, dialing 911 on your cellular phone won't help you. But knowing how to properly apply a pulley rein will. The pulley rein can stop a horse faster than antilock brakes when used correctly. But it's a very harsh rein aid for emergency situations only. *The pulley rein has no place in normal school riding.*

With a runaway, the sooner you regain control, the better. A horse that's allowed to stretch out like a race horse and take off at a gallop is very hard to stop. Remember, if you stop the boulder before it starts rolling down that hill, it can't go anywhere.

But let's say you didn't stop the boulder quite soon enough, that you're riding in a large ring, the wind whips up, Watergate is feeling

Aids to the Pulley Rein

1. Transfer the reins into your right hand, and then slide your *left* hand over both reins, two-thirds of the way up Watergate's mane (**a**).
2. Get into a modified half seat: you lift yourself forward and out of the seat a bit. (See lesson 7 for more about the half seat.)
3. With your right hand, grasp the right rein as close to the bit as you can without unbalancing yourself. Continue to hold both reins in your left hand (**b**).
4. Now you're going to do something similar to what you do to start a lawn mower. It's critical. Support your weight into the left rein and on Watergate's neck, and with that right hand, *jerk* by twisting your shoulders until they are parallel with the horse. If your lawn mower is like mine, you'll have to pull very hard. Your body weight will be driven backwards, preparing you for a sudden stop (**c**).

a

Obviously, you can't really practice this on a horse that isn't running away, because it wouldn't be very nice to the horse. But you can go through the motions of gathering up the reins and doing everything but the harsh *jerk* so that if you ever need to use a pulley rein, you'll be prepared.

frisky anyway, and he suddenly decides to bolt down the long side of the ring.

First, *if you're carrying a crop, drop it fast!* Actually, you should have sensed that Watergate was getting frisky and dropped the crop long ago. But if you still have it, let it slide out of your hand. Don't lift your hand or let go of a rein to get rid of the crop.

Now you must use your body weight in such a way that Watergate's mouth becomes a pulley. Assuming you're right handed, the goal is to get your right hand on the rein as near to the bit as you can before you pull. To do that takes some finesse, however.

b

c

Bending the Horse

Bending is one of the most basic skills for effectively controlling the horse. If your horse doesn't bend in a corner, he becomes unbalanced. You'll probably get away with it 9 out of 10 times, 99 out of 100, or even 999 out of 1,000, but sooner or later you and your unbalanced horse are going to fall. So fix the problem before it happens: Practice bending the horse until it becomes automatic.

Left- and Right-Handed Horses

Be aware that a horse may be left or right handed and that almost all horses are stiff on one side. The only way to fix this is by exercising the stiff side.

In bending your horse, how you use your legs, the intensity with which you use them, and your timing are all important. (You don't want the horse to speed up every time you use your leg.)

To bend your horse, apply your inside leg at the girth. In this context, "girth" has nothing to do with where the actual saddle strap is; it's where your legs should fall when you're properly balanced. Because horses move away from pressure, your horse should move the middle part of his body — the part you're sitting on — away from your inside leg. At the same time, his head should be looking to the inside, but only just enough for you to see the corner of his inside eye.

Place your outside leg back, behind the girth, as a guard to keep the horse from moving his entire body away from the inside leg. This is important. Horses are also taught to move laterally with leg pressure. Moving your outside leg back will let your horse know you want him to bend.

At the same time, close one hand and open the other to a corresponding degree. Think of it as shaping the horse to the degree of the turn. No one can tell you how much to pull on this hand or that; it depends on the horse, and you've got to feel this yourself. Remember, though, that whenever you use your inside leg, the pressure is received in your outside hand.

Before continuing, review the aids you use to bend the horse.

Aids to Bending the Horse

1. Position your inside leg at the girth (this is your active leg).
2. Position your outside leg behind the girth.
3. Sit on your inside seat bone.
4. Turn your shoulders toward the bend and to the degree of bend.
5. Create the bend with your inside hand, and give equally with your outside hand.

◀

When you bend a horse, you use your inside leg toward your outside hand.

Complex? Yes. Important? Yes. You must understand this concept. You are trying to keep the horse upright and square on all four feet so he doesn't slip. The idea is that all four feet have equal weight above them at all times. You do not want to be riding a horse that's careening around a corner with the only bearing surface being the side of his shoes or hooves. Think about why trains use connected boxcars instead of one long car. They can't lean around a corner, because they would fall over. It's the joints between cars that get trains around corners. Your horse is jointed, too, and you must bend him to get him around the corner.

More on Using Your Hands

You learned in lesson 1 the basic position for holding the reins, with your elbows bent and your hands two inches directly above the withers and four inches apart. A straight line should run from your elbows, through your wrist, to the horse's mouth.

But there's much more to learn about hand position and controls. Your hands determine about one-third of your control over a horse. You must be able to keep them still and prevent them from bouncing. One way to do this is to hold your shoulders back and down. Most people with bouncing hands either have a violently bouncing seat or carry their shoulders pinched up. (If the latter, your shoulder muscles will hurt.)

Hold your hands so that your fingernails point toward your stomach, and keep them more open than closed. Most people try to hold the reins in their hands by forming a fist, but if you tighten up your fingers on the reins, you tighten your forearms and then your back, causing your hands to bounce. What holds the reins in your hands is the pressure between your thumbs and forefingers. From the your index finger down, each successive finger is graded out just a tiny bit more.

Progression of Hand Aids

The action of closing your hands on the reins is an aid. Like all the other aids, hand aids can be used in a progression. The following are listed in ascending order of severity:

1. Press your thumbs against your index fingers.
2. If no response: Align your fingers straight up and down. (Pull your bottom fingers in line with your index finger.)
3. If no response: Close your fingers around the reins. (Make a fist.)
4. If no response: Close your wrists. (Cock them in slightly.)
5. If no response: Bring your hands in toward your body, working from your elbows.
6. If no response: Pull your hands straight back, using your whole arm.

Fine Control

As with any other aids, if you resort to the harshest hand aid first, you've lost any fine control you might otherwise have by using them progressively. Generally, hand aids are used with a direct rein aid.

We can also use the hand aids to ask for a downward transition, and that's how I'd like you to practice them. So ask Watergate to trot, and then ask him to slow down to a walk.

The first time you try this, use thumb/forefinger pressure, the gentlest hand aid. Watergate should slow down. Ask him to trot again, and this time try pulling in your bottom fingers. Watergate probably stopped.

The point? If the first hand aid you try doesn't prompt your horse to respond as you want, try the next most harsh aid, but if thumb/forefinger pressure worked, you don't need to go further.

Even more important to the learning process is the ability to feel the difference in Watergate's responses. In mastering this skill, you will understand that there's a long way between the first and last hand aids. *Always use the mildest aid that achieves the desired result.* In other words, use the aids in progression.

Setting Your Hands

As you learned in lesson 1, you can also use your hands by setting them, so that they don't move or give. In contrast, if you flex your fingers in response to pressure from the horse's mouth, your hand is passive. When you get to the canter in lesson 7, you'll understand why knowing the difference is important.

Remember, there are infinite positions between a set hand and a passive hand; it's all a matter of degree. If you're asking, "How fixed or passive should my hands be?" I'd say no one can answer that question for you. As always, use the mildest aid you can to get the desired result.

Height of Your Hands

The height of your hands also makes a difference. The lower your hands go, or the closer they are to the withers, the longer the horse's stride will be. Generally, the higher your hands, the shorter the horse's stride.

Try this. Ask Watergate to pick up a nice trot. You will post. Place your hands closer to the withers. Make your hands passive, giving to his mouth. Watergate's stride should feel a bit longer. This technique will prove useful in future lessons when you ask a horse to yield to your leg, that is, move forward more aggressively.

Now raise your hands higher above the withers and set them. Can you feel a difference in Watergate's stride? Watergate's gait should feel shorter and choppier.

More on Using Your Legs

When I say "leg," I mean from your uppermost calf down to the point of your heel. On some sensitive horses, however, your thighs might be considered part of the leg.

There are two distinct ways to use your legs — slapping and squeezing — with infinite nuances between. A slapping leg can be used with every stride, twice a stride, or, indeed, as fast as you can apply. It will tend to make your horse step higher and shorter. In contrast, squeezing will tend to make your horse move forward with a longer stride.

Squeezing, by the way, does not mean clamping. An important rule in riding is this: *Steady pressure on a horse won't work.* So when I say squeeze, I mean close your legs more strongly and then release. Close, then release. But do not clamp.

Part and Position

The part of your leg you use and your leg position also make a difference. The farther down the leg, the more aggressive the aid. If you squeeze with your heels, you'll get more reaction than squeezing with your upper calves.

The two basic leg positions are at the girth and behind the girth. In case you've forgotten, positioning your legs "at the girth" means at the perfect center balance of the horse, where you should be sitting, with ears, shoulders, hips, and heels in line (**a**). It doesn't mean you should line up your leg with the saddle's belly strap. Except for an extreme correction, "behind the girth" means from two to four inches behind where your legs naturally hang (**b**). Here again, there are infinite degrees and nuances in the way you use your legs behind the girth, but in general the farther back you place a leg, the more aggressive the leg aid.

RULES OF RIDING

Steady pressure on a horse won't work.

◄

When your legs hang at the perfect center balance of the horse, they are positioned at the girth (a). The farther behind the girth they are positioned, the more aggressive the leg aid (b).

Try out these different leg positions on Watergate. Ask him to trot, and then ask him to move on by squeezing at the girth. Slow him down a bit with a half halt. Ask him again to move faster by squeezing behind the girth. Feel a difference?

Seat Aids

Despite the risk of information overload in this lesson, let me add the three basic seat positions to the list of aids:

- Very light (restrictive) seat — you arch your lower back slightly, with your hips forward.
- Normal seat — your hips are straight up and down.
- Driving seat — you roll back the top part of your hips, or your pelvis, as if you were trying to sit on your back pants pockets. You drive the horse forward with your seat.

A very light seat will tend to make your horse's stride short and choppy. A very driving seat will tend to make your horse move long and low.

Just to make your life a bit more complex, which seat bone you sit on also matters. Horses move away from pressure and weight. (Well, most do.) So if you sit on your left seat bone with a very driving seat, the horse should move to the right in a long, low fashion. Conversely, if you maintain a very light, or restrictive, seat while sitting on your right seat bone, your horse would move to the left, but with a shortened, choppier gait.

When I was first learning to ride, I had some of the best instructors that money could buy — the Army paid for them — and I just didn't believe all this stuff about how your seat worked. Using your legs and your reins was easy to understand, but I just wasn't convinced the horse could feel what I did with my seat bones. Even when my instructors were able to make my horse do things I couldn't. I was convinced they had some sort of magic pill. But as I took more and more lessons, I learned that what I did with my seat really did matter, even with untrained horses.

So think a bit more about the effect of your seat. A horse weighs an average of 1,000 pounds and you weigh — I'll give you a break here — say, 100 pounds. The ratio is 10 to 1. If you carry a 10-pound knapsack around for an hour, you'll find during your hike that if the pack is heavier on one side than the other, you'll change your position to distribute the weight more evenly. If it's true for you, why not for a horse with a rider on his back?

Progressive Halt

This lesson has offered you much more information about the aids, and now you should be able to see how, with experience, the progression of the aids becomes much more complex and precise.

For example, consider how the progression of the aids applies to another technique, the progressive halt.

Get Watergate going at a good trot and then give him the aids to halt, starting with the mildest and progressing as needed. This will be something like slowing a 16-speed truck; you don't have to use every gear (aid) when downshifting — you can use only those you know you need.

The pure and simple aids to the halt (with some added explanation) are:

Aids to the Halt

1. Sit down. You don't just sit down, you drive with your back. In other words, you rotate the top of your hips toward your back pockets, but not so much that your feet come forward.
2. Set your hands. Stiffen them by pushing thumbs onto forefingers. Your hands do not give to pressure.
3. Squeeze with your legs. Use your very upper calves in an elongated squeezing action.
4. Push with your back into your hands. From your driving seat, bring the top of your hips farther back, collapsing your spinal column. (When I say collapsing your spinal column, I don't mean letting it slide under the rib cage.)

You have just pushed with your back into your hands, providing a forward impulse. It may seem odd to be **driving** Watergate forward when trying to make him stop. But remember, you're *driving him into your hands*. This increases rein pressure more effectively than pulling your hands back.

Rein Pressure

There are two ways to get rein pressure, or get the bit to close in your horse's mouth: You either pull back your hands, which at best is ineffective, or you can drive him forward, forcing him to close the bit on himself. The latter works better.

Why doesn't pulling back on the reins work very well? First of all, you're using only one-third or less of the control you have over the horse by depending exclusively on the reins. The horse can evade the rein aid simply by inverting his back, sticking out his nose, and raising his head. You end up pulling on his back teeth, which won't slow him. The whole purpose of the aids is to prevent this kind of evasion from occurring. (You'll learn more about evasions in the next lesson.)

What to do if . . . the horse still isn't stopping.

He's not running away with you, he's just not stopping easily. So make the aids more severe. But remember, pulling back on the reins is not going to get you anywhere.

Try raising and bringing your hands in toward your body a bit, closing your fingers, and cocking your wrists slightly. Take a very extreme forward posture with your back: Pull your legs back four inches from the girth, slap with your legs, and then collapse and stiffen your back. Can you see how this is all much harsher than the original set of aids?

What to do if . . . the horse still isn't stopping.

You need to get results, so try a modified pulley rein. Instead of positioning your hands two-thirds of the way up the horse's neck, modify the pulley rein by holding your hands *at the withers*. This action is not as severe as a traditional pulley rein.

If that doesn't work, go straight to a full-blown pulley rein, and I guarantee you that you'll get a result.

You're on track if you can:

- ✓ Cite the aids to the halt, walk, and trot. (Extra kudos if you can also cite the aids to bend and add impulsion to the walk and trot.)
- ✓ Explain how a jointed snaffle bit works and how it differs from a leverage bit.
- ✓ Demonstrate each of the five basic rein aids.
- ✓ Bring your horse to a halt using the proper aids.
- ✓ With increasing frequency, select the mildest rein aid that achieves the desired result.
- ✓ Increasingly use your legs, back, and hands together when employing all aids, no matter how minor.

Riding Is a Fine Art

Don't expect to remember, let alone apply, all the information in this lesson any time soon. But it's important to realize that learning to really control a horse is a fine art. Do you need all this detail for a trail ride? Absolutely not. For training a horse? Probably not. To get the very best performance out of your horse? Absolutely so.

Think of riding as a giant combination lock. Now calculate all the possibilities. You have five rein aids, three hand heights (high, normal, and low), and six distinct ways to use your hands. You have two basic leg positions (at the girth and behind, with innumerable gradations), and two basic ways to use your legs (slapping or squeezing), either independently or together, and from the top of your calves to your heels. There are three seat positions (driving, passive, and light), and with each of these postures your back can either encourage or restrict motion.

I'm not a mathematician, but it would be impossible to pick a lock with so many permutations. But in essence that's what you're trying to do when you ride a horse. So should you give up riding right now because there's no way to pick the lock? No. For now, if X doesn't work, try Y. If that combination doesn't work, try another. You'll never run out of combinations. And you'll be a much better rider if I've convinced you that to learn to ride well, you must *think*.

With my students I like to use another analogy. When learning to drive, you have to think about using the turn signal when you approach a corner. But it soon becomes automatic, and soon your riding aids will, too. Getting to that point takes practice, practice, practice. Meanwhile, always try to use the most complete aid that you possibly can, incorporating the necessary nuances with hands, legs, seat, and back.

Half Halt, On the Bit, and Evasions

IN THIS LESSON, you're going to read about three additional ways to control your horse. One way is through the **half halt**. Another is to **collect** your horse, also known as getting your horse onto the bit. A third is by learning to handle **evasions** — that is, when a horse doesn't do what you ask or develops bad habits to avoid work.

For this lesson, your instructor may saddle you with a horse that is particularly likely to evade. At my barn, that horse is Waffle.

Waffle

AGE: 14
WEIGHT: About 1,200 lbs. (She's too fat.)
SIZE: 15 hands

BREED: Draft Cross
COLOR: Strawberry Roan, Star

Waffle is a cross between a Quarter Horse and a type of Draft known as a Belgian — hence the name (Belgian) Waffle. She reigns as queen of the pasture. Don't dare try to give another horse a carrot without taking one along for her. If you do, she'll run all the other horses off and grab the treat.

She also hates for the shutters on her stall to be closed. If she hears you coming with food and the shutter is closed, she'll knock it open and knock you over with the force of a gale wind.

Under saddle, she has evasions down to a science. She's figured out very well what the rider will and will not allow, and she'll test you at every turn. She'll make you want to drop riding and take up golf. But then, miraculously, she'll give you a beautiful ride. Her fantastic conformation makes her a very smooth mount. Why does she behave like this? She's really a very talented horse, but extremely lazy.

Hip Strengthener

This exercise strengthens the muscles that support your hips, which come in handy for posting or anything else that requires rising out of the saddle.

Lie on the floor on your back with one knee bent and one leg straight. Make a fist with each hand, and with palms facing down, slide fists under your buttocks. (This protects your lower back and helps keep it on the floor.) Your head also should remain on the floor.

Lift your straight leg as high as the top of the bent knee, and then lower it. Now reverse your legs and repeat. Take it slow. Do only a few at first. Gradually build up your strength.

The Half Halt

Previously, in lesson 3, you learned that a half halt is just what it sounds like: It's half a halt and can be used to slow down a horse. But the half halt also serves another very important purpose: to let the horse know you're going to ask her to do something different, such as pick up a different gait or turn a corner. *The half halt is one of the most important aids that you will use.*

To understand the half halt, think of it as equivalent to clearing your throat or raising your hand to get someone's attention. It primes the person to receive your message. With a horse, you use the half halt to say, "Waffle, pay attention, I'm going to give a new command now." Or sometimes, "Waffle, I know what you're thinking about doing and want you to cut it out."

To further understand the half halt, first review the basic aids to the halt:

Aids to Halt

1. Sit down.
2. Set your hands.
3. Close your legs on the horse.
4. Push with your back into your hands.

How you execute the half halt depends on the desired result. In other words, it can be very, very mild or very, very harsh. Choosing the intensity comes under the heading of "horseman's tact." This is something you learn over time while riding and will vary with the horse's personality.

During one lap around the ring, good riders will always give at least eight half halts. How is this possible? Because there are four corners in a ring. There's a half halt before you enter the corner to create a bend, and a half halt after the corner, to straighten the horse. Obviously, since there are four corners, that equals eight half halts. But practically speaking, eight is a small number.

In a small ring — say, 60 by 120 feet — a professional rider probably will give 30 to 40 half halts in one lap. Why? Because before each command he prefaces it by a half halt to get the horse's attention.

Try this out. Ask Waffle to trot around the ring. Think ahead! Before you ask her to bend around the corner, give her a half halt. Now around the corner you go. As you come out of the corner, half halt again before you ask her to straighten out.

Practice your half halts at the corners going both ways around the ring. If you practice enough, half halts, too, will become as natural as using the turn signal when your car approaches a corner.

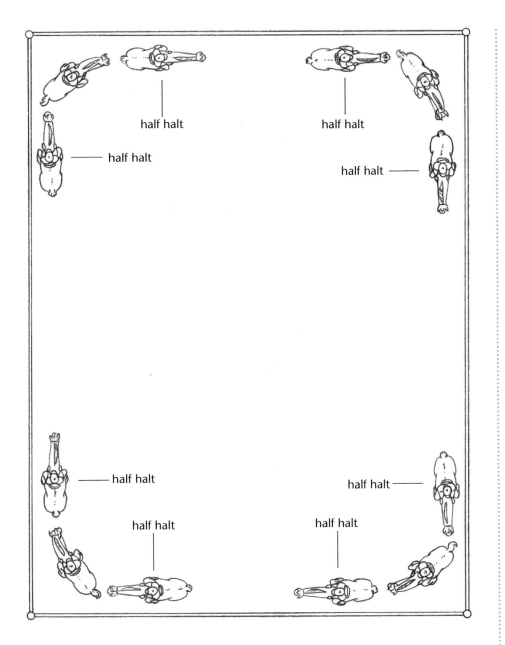

half halt

half halt

half halt

half halt

half halt

half halt

half halt

half halt

◀

You should use the half halt a minimum of eight times in one lap around the ring.

Collection: On the Bit

On the bit, or collection, can best be described as a posture. It involves getting the horse into a posture that will better enable us to direct her. Learning collection is so important to advancing your riding skills that I'm going to describe it a couple of different ways to make sure you understand.

First, consider how much a person's posture can reveal. We can all spot lazy people. Their shoulders slump, their eyes are dull, they have little interest in their surroundings, and, if you ask them to do something, they drag their feet. Compare that to people who hold their shoulders back, look alert, show interest in their surroundings, and have a spring in their step. They are ready to meet the next challenge.

The same is true with horses. So what posture do you want Waffle to have? You want her standing proud, with a twinkle in her eye. You want her interested in her surroundings and ready to move forward. That's collection.

Another way to describe collection involves agility. Take that most agile of animals, the cat. Why can a cat jump to a kitchen countertop? Because his anatomy is such that by rounding his back, he can put his back feet in front of his front feet. The horse, of course, can't put her back feet in front and spring onto a counter, but the more rounded her back, the more agile she becomes.

Is Collection Always Necessary?

Collection is always necessary to some degree, because it facilitates greater control.

There's a rule in riding: *The horse must always be between your hands and your legs.* This means that if you ever cease using your hands, the horse should immediately and minutely move ahead faster; should you stop using your legs, the horse should immediately and minutely slow down. If this doesn't happen, you're not in sufficient control.

Further along in the book you'll learn how greater degrees of collection come into play. For now, start noticing the difference between a collected horse and one that isn't.

To collect Waffle, ask her to round her back. Set your hands and drive her with your legs into your hands. In this instance, Waffle becomes a shorter package, because the energy you're asking her for can't be projected forward. It must go somewhere, so it becomes contained, or collected, and Waffle assumes a more agile posture, with her hind legs tracking farther underneath her and carrying more weight.

▶

To collect your horse, set your hands, and drive with your seat and legs into your hands.

Evasions

Unfortunately, horses pick up bad habits, or evasions. An evasion occurs any time a trained horse wants to do something other than what you ask. This can range from going faster when you're heading toward the barn, to bucking you off.

You can correct most evasions simply by redirecting the horse's thinking. You do that with a half halt and then a corrective command.

To correct an evasion, you also need a reasonably good seat and sitting trot, knowledge of your rein aids, and confidence in your ability as a rider. Confidence is the key word here. *You can't correct a horse if you doubt that you can.* This is especially important with a smart horse like Waffle. You have to be a smart rider to ride a smart horse successfully. You have to get inside her head, not just sit pensively on top of her.

I won't bore you by listing all the individual evasions and combinations you may encounter. Besides, I can't give you the exact solutions for all horses, because I don't know them all. Understand that when evasions occur, many factors come into play, such as how the horse was trained initially, the bit you're using, and your level of riding skill. You should ask your instructor for specific instructions on handling this or that evasion in your particular horse.

Why Does a Horse Evade?

Horses are much like people. They have personalities, brains, and all five senses. They may not feel as good on some days as others. They have emotional attachments. They may miss an old friend that has passed on. They can even become depressed.

All these factors can contribute to evasions, making them worse on some days than others. And some days, horses just don't want to go to work. Just like people.

However, to give you a better idea of what advice your instructor might offer, I'll cite some of the common evasions and provide some common fixes. Except for "popping the shoulder," which is one of the most common evasions you'll encounter, my fixes are brief and blunt.

I discuss these evasions, by the way, in their order of severity. Except for the most extreme evasions, such as bucking or rearing, all horses — yup, folks, all horses — will demonstrate these behaviors from time to time.

Popping the Shoulder

While trotting around the ring, you decide to turn Waffle left to cut across the middle. You give her the aids and she turns her head to the inside like a good mare, but her body moves to the outside, away from where you want to turn. What's she doing? "Popping" her outside shoulder.

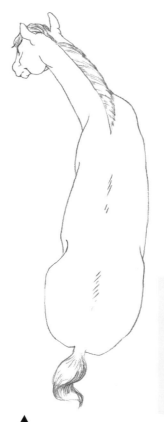

This horse is popping her right shoulder.

She's trying to move to the outside, following her shoulder, because she doesn't want to make that turn.

The shoulder is the leading part of the horse. Meanwhile, her head is turned so much to the inside that it's beyond her inside shoulder. (No, horses don't *have* to follow their heads.) Either Waffle is just trying to get out of work or she wants to go someplace other than where you had in mind. She might be trying to drift back toward the barn.

Your initial reaction, probably, is to pull her head more to the inside. How does Waffle respond? She continues to travel to the outside, following that shoulder. You must refocus her attention.

First, straighten Waffle out and continue around the ring. Then assume she's going to try popping her shoulder again when you ask her to turn. Prepare to use the following aids:

Aids for Preventing a Popped Shoulder

1. Position the outside rein as an indirect rein behind the withers.
2. Position your outside leg at the girth sharply.
3. Put weight on your inside seat bone.
4. Keep the inside rein passive, as an indirect rein in front of the withers. In other words, the *outside rein overrides the inside rein.*

Yes, this adds up to a complex maneuver, but if you prevent the shoulder from popping, you'll get the turn. Realize you are using rein aids differently than you normally would with a horse that doesn't pop her shoulder. You must anticipate the problem and prevent it. Anticipating problems is crucial to riding well.

How does the half halt fit in here? Before you reach where you want to turn, you would use a half halt to get Waffle's attention, to let her know you're going to give a command and to stop her from thinking about popping her shoulder. However, if she's already popped her shoulder and you missed it, it's too late to half halt her; now you must straighten her out and try again.

Snatching at the Reins

You've got to figure out if this is a physical or a mental problem, and that can be difficult to do. I'd estimate that about 6 out of 10 times, it's physical. The horse may have problems with her teeth, such as *wolf teeth* (teeth that emerge in front of the back teeth and interfere with the bit). She may have tears in the cheek or gum, or the bit might not fit properly. It could even be allergies.

If your school horse tosses her head, you need to discuss it with your instructor. In the case of Waffle, I can assure you the problem is mental, not physical.

Your first reaction will be to snatch back at the reins. A correction is in order, but punishing Waffle with your hands will only propagate the problem. Over the long term, it will make her gums calloused, leaving her hard mouthed and even better able to evade you by snatching at the reins.

Other ways to correct Waffle would be to tap her with a whip or crop or give her a short, sharp kick with your heels or spurs. It's unlikely you'll be using spurs at this stage of your riding. My druthers would be to use a whip for this evasion, but that could make a horse go faster and may not be the best option for you. So again, you need to work with your instructor if you encounter this problem.

Lowering the Head and Shoveling Out the Nose

A horse that lowers her head and shovels out her nose may be signaling a physical problem, even more so than by snatching the reins. A principal cause is a sore back. In fact, I think more horses experience sore backs than many people realize. Unfortunately, diagnosing back problems is very difficult. But if your horse lowers her head and shovels out her nose, the problem needs the attention of your instructor and the stable veterinarian.

If physical problems have been ruled out, you need to think more about how the bit works in the horse's mouth before attempting to correct this evasion. Understand that pulling back on the reins will not fix the problem. Because the horse has her head down and her nose out, pulling back simply forces the bit against the back teeth and, as you already know, steady pressure doesn't work on a horse. Instead, use the sides of the bit. Pull *one* rein back toward the hip. This is a punishment. The sharper the pull (or jerk), the more effective the result. If the horse didn't get the message, repeat the punishment.

▶ *This horse is lowering her head and shoveling out her nose.*

Inversion

Well, Waffle's latest ploy is raising her head higher than normal and sticking her nose out again. She's trying another way to keep the bit from working on her bars. Physical discomfort, fear, or poor training can cause this problem, but in Waffle's case, we know it's mental.

To better understand what's happening, visualize a very collected (rounded) parade horse. It has a very compact posture, whereas a horse running a race has an elongated posture. Do you want to ride a race horse or a collected parade horse? I strongly recommend the latter. It's the degree of the roundness that determines the amount of collection and how much the hind legs track under the horse.

How does this apply to an inverted horse? Get her to round her back, which, incidentally, is the only way to ride a horse comfortably.

You must drive Waffle forward into your hands, but here comes the rub: Most beginners take what I just said to mean you pull your hands back to your hips. Instead, use your legs to push into your hands.

► *An inverted horse is trying to keep the bit from working on her bars.*

Correcting an Inverted Horse

Here's a simple exercise to help correct an inverted horse: Use the aids for backing up. Sit down, set your hands, squeeze with your legs, and push with your back *into and beyond your hands*.

Let me repeat what "beyond" means. It does not mean "pull on the reins." When a horse is inverted, you can't pull the head down or the nose back. This only creates more resistance. It's a futile approach! By closing your legs and creating the impulse to go forward, you are driving her from the rear toward the front as opposed to pulling the front toward the rear. Driving her forward from the rear will tend to make her back up. You'll feel the reins tighten, but it's important that you be able to swear that you didn't pull on them to correct the inversion.

What to do if . . . the horse bends the wrong way and her body is cockeyed.

It's pretty hard for a perfectly straight horse to evade. There's a moral here: Keep your horse straight. Go straight to where you're traveling, with your horse's hind feet tracking exactly behind her front feet.

What to do if . . . the horse is running away.

Prevent this from happening! Nothing's going to protect you if you trample a bee's nest, a plane crashes, or aliens land in the paddock. But you can almost always prevent a horse from running away simply by paying attention. The second she speeds up faster than you want her to, half halt her. More about handling the runaway appears in lesson 8.

What to do if . . . the horse won't move forward.

School horses usually stop or stand still when given conflicting or confusing signals, which beats having them run away, buck, or rear. A school horse has learned that when you inadvertently kick her, you didn't really mean for her to gallop off into the sunset.

Learning to ride under these circumstances may require you to use much more leg and, sometimes, a crop to keep the horse moving forward. If, however, you are becoming frustrated riding school horses, the solution may be to move up to the next level of horse. But I'll always err on the safe side with a beginning rider, and you'll never go wrong by learning the workings of a school horse.

What to do if . . . the horse is spoiled.

Okay, your horse is spoiled. She occasionally swishes her tail or lays back her ears when you give her an aid. On one of her bad days she'll make ugly faces at the other horses in your class. Most barns have a spoiled horse or two and you'll need to learn to deal with them. On the plus side, such horses can help teach you how to handle evasions.

However, if such behavior becomes commonplace, discuss it with your instructor. You need a good ride every now and then to keep up your enthusiasm.

What to do if . . . the horse rears.

When most horses rear, they rear with a bend to the left or the right. If your horse rears to the left, pull the left rein out with an extreme leading rein to the left and drive her forward. If she rears with a bend to the right, do the same, but with the right rein to the right side.

It is absolutely imperative that you do not try to keep your balance with the reins. Do not pull straight back. You could pull her over backwards, on top of you.

Rearing is the most dangerous of all evasions, and if you ride a horse that rears, you should refuse to ride the horse ever again.

RULES OF RIDING

Rearing is the most dangerous of all evasions. Refuse to ride any horse that rears.

What to do if . . . the horse bucks.

This shouldn't happen in a school horse, but maybe the weather suddenly changed and there's excitement in the air, or maybe other horses started running around and your horse decides she wants to kick up her heels.

Earlier in this chapter, I told you that an inverted posture is bad. But in this instance, inversion is good. Picture Saturday afternoon at the rodeo. The bucking horse has her back rounded and her head down. The cowboy is desperately trying to stay on.

If you are riding a horse that bucks, invert, invert! Get her head up, using an indirect rein and a jerk if you have to. The horse has more trouble bucking if her nose is above the point of the shoulder, so do anything necessary to raise it. Then get the horse moving forward immediately.

▶

If a horse bucks or kicks out with her back legs, get her moving forward.

You're on track if you can:

✓ Issue a half halt using the proper complement of aids instead of just your hands.
✓ Use the half halt whenever you're about to tell the horse to do something.
✓ Collect a horse.
✓ Use the proper aids to correct a horse that pops its shoulder.

┌─ Evasions vs. Amusements ─┐

An evasion is something horses do to avoid doing what riders ask. There are other things that mounted horses do for their own self amusement, such as eating grass, grabbing leaves off a tree, or playing in the water trough. This can mean a lack of respect for the rider. But if you adequately communicate with your horse and her thinking, she will respect you and be less likely to try to amuse herself.

Half Seat and Introduction to the Canter

The half seat also is known as the jumping position or the **two-point seat**. Yes, I said jumping. Soon, you're going to go out onto the trail, which isn't really as flat as you might have thought, especially on a horse. You must learn how to take little jumps over fallen trees or streams and how to ride at higher speeds. The half seat can help you do that more easily and securely. With the help of the half seat, you're also going to learn how to canter in this lesson.

A good horse for this outing would be Sampson.

Sampson

AGE: 10
WEIGHT: 1,300 lbs.
SIZE: 16.2 hands

BREED: American
    Cream Draft
COLOR: Palomino

Sampson has an especially humorous personality. He likes to lick the back of the *farrier's* head when getting trimmed and reshod. He likes to rough-and-tumble with other horses in the field and to box with them while standing on his hind legs. That's why he's in a pasture reserved for the "bad boys." These horses aren't really bad, they're just a very silly, especially rambunctious group, so we keep them together instead of with other horses that might not be able to tolerate their antics.

Sampson is perhaps best known for his love of watermelon. If you're picnicking with watermelon and he's free-grazing nearby, watch out. He'll knock over the table, and you, to get to it.

Under saddle, Sampson has an unusual habit. He squeals like a pig, which is his way of complaining when you ask him to do something. But he's very safe and actually a bit lazy, despite his size. You'll definitely need the mounting block. But remember, you can't judge a horse's temperament by his size, and it's clear that, like Toby, Sampson is another gentle giant.

The Half Seat

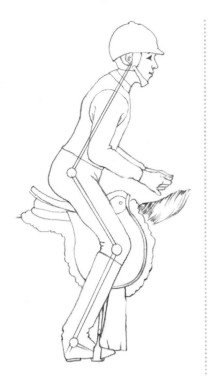

▲
The key to the half seat is keeping your joints flexed, which will help absorb the shock when jumping.

Just as a half halt is half a halt, a half seat is half a seat. You aren't sitting fully down into the saddle. To learn the half seat position, it will help if you study the posture you assume when jumping off something, such as a low porch. You don't jump off a porch with your back and legs stiff and straight. It'll hurt. Instead, applying basic physics, you bend slightly forward so that your back, knees, and ankles flex to absorb the shock. You do likewise with the half seat.

Ask Sampson to trot around the ring and take the half seat position. Keep him moving straight and forward. When his feet hit the ground, flex your joints and absorb the shock.

You must find the proper balance, and your hands are integral to this; they should be halfway up the horse's neck, more or less underneath your forehead. You should feel as though your body is staying at the same level, in the same place, as the horse moves underneath you, with only your joints adjusting to Sampson's movement. You should feel your calves flexing: They will flex down for just a moment, then release as you follow along.

If you can't feel your upper calves against Sampson's side, turn your toes out *slightly*. (Having bowed legs would help the half seat come easily.)

A Note to Your Instructor

I teach students to canter in half seat. I've found that the bouncing of the canter can upset both horse and rider. Half seat enables riders to better absorb the shock while they start to feel the motion of the canter. I only use half seat, however, until riders become comfortable with the concept of cantering. Then I have them begin using the full balanced (sitting) seat.

Cantering

Cantering is one of the most exciting, most exhilarating, and scariest gaits to learn. It is a three beat gait. (See illustration on page 77.) It's smoother than the trot but there is a lot more motion, and it's twice as fast. You're going to be traveling at a whopping 13 miles an hour or so. But right now, you must listen to my directions. I say this because once you start the canter, you won't hear a word I say.

Leave your crop behind, and begin by asking Sampson to trot. You should be in half seat. Keep your heels down and get Sampson going straight. Look ahead, right between Sampson's ears, and decide exactly where you intend to ask him to canter. Picking a spot will help you give Sampson a clearer, correctly timed message. Otherwise, Sampson is likely to stretch into a faster trot, which creates a bumpy ride and could very well unseat you. Now, half halt, and then apply these aids:

Aids to the Canter

1. Sit down.

2. Position your inside leg at the girth.

3. Position your outside leg behind the girth.

4. Hold the inside rein shorter than the outside rein, but both with equal contact.

5. Squeeze with your outside leg.

6. Push with your back.

7. Give with your hands.

Use these aids exactly in sequence, and all within about one-tenth of a second.

Okay, let's try it this way: Hold onto the mane and kick until Sampson canters. (Also, be advised that "Whoa" can sound an awful lot like "Go!")

The truth of the matter is that I don't want you worrying at this point about using the aids to the canter. I'll return to them in lesson 9. For now, I want you to concentrate on controlling the horse and your position at this new, faster gait. Grab the mane and kick as you trot, and Sampson will pick up the canter.

Once you get Sampson going, canter for about 10 or 15 strides, and then come back down to the trot. Let go of the mane and gently pull back on the reins. Practice over and over and over until you can smoothly enter the canter and maintain a straight trajectory.

Eventually, you'll learn to use the proper aids to the canter, which will give you more control over your horse, and enable you to canter with finesse and in greater comfort. But right now, there are other fundamentals to learn about this gait.

1   2   2   3   (suspended in air)

Cantering Tip

If you don't pick a spot and give a clear, correctly timed message, your horse is likely to stretch into a faster trot. You'll have a bumpy ride and could very well become unseated. So plan ahead.

▲
The canter is a three-beat gait, which means the horse's feet strike the ground three times in one stride.

Quadriceps Strengthener

Half seat requires strong legs, and this leg exercise will work on your quadriceps, the four muscles in the front of each thigh. While standing with your hands on your hips, place your feet hip width apart, your toes facing forward.

Keeping your back straight and lifted, slowly lower your buttocks behind you, as if you were going to sit in a chair. If you can, stretch your arms out in front of you. If this is difficult, place your hands on your hips or out to the sides. Slowly rise to standing and repeat. Throughout the exercise keep your stomach muscles tight and your weight in your heels. If you bend straight down and don't sit backward somewhat, it could create pressure on your knees.

The Canter Seat

To understand the canter seat, you need to realize what's happening underneath you. As I explained before, the horse is moving in a three-beat gait. As a result, he's going to move your body in a very unique way.

First, work toward sitting down at the canter. Begin by trying not to hold onto the mane. When you're comfortable, try to hold yourself increasingly upright while you canter, until you're actually sitting in the saddle. Now you can *really* learn to canter.

Your body is being moved forward one hip at a time, in a twisting motion. It's natural to feel a need to "scrub," or slide across, the saddle in response, but don't. Remember that weight and its distribution has a large effect on the horse. You want to stay centered and avoid getting your teeth rattled

As with the sitting trot, tension at the canter works against you. However, now you have to learn a different way of using your back. Instead of adopting a forward and backward motion, as with the sitting trot, you have to roll your hips in time with the motion of the canter. Collapse your spinal column and go down with the saddle, and then straighten your back as the saddle rises.

This is when most students want to shorten their stirrups. They think this will give them better balance, but instead they lose that nice low base and center of gravity, which they really need to sit to the canter. If you feel a need to shorten your stirrups, you're probably trying to stand up in them. This is incorrect. So resist the temptation and refocus on maintaining that correct balanced seat.

What to do if . . . your horse trots faster instead of cantering.

This usually occurs because your aids were ill timed or because you didn't have enough contained energy when giving the aids to initiate the canter.

On timing: The most important thing to do is remember the sequence of the aids. Then always pick a specific spot where you'll initiate the canter. This is very, very important. But don't focus on the spot. Instead, just pick one and then look at where you're going.

Contained energy means the horse is between your legs and your hands. Remember this simple test? If you ever cease using your hands and they go loose, the horse should immediately and minutely go forward (faster), and should you ever cease using your legs, the horse should immediately and minutely slow down. At all times when you're school riding (but not necessarily when you're trail riding), the horse should be balanced between your legs and hands.

Building Energy

Cantering a calm horse — the kind you should be mounted on for these lessons — is somewhat like burning rubber at a stoplight.

Just in case you didn't do this in high school, here's how: You put the car in neutral, rev the engine, wait for the green light, at which point you slip the transmission into drive and jam the gas pedal down as far as it will go.

How does this apply to cantering? Just before you canter, you have to rev the horse's engine. That doesn't mean you'll go faster, but that the contained energy will increase. The horse should be struggling to go faster, but you're containing that energy by restraining him. When you reach the point that you picked out to start the canter, you put him into drive. That is, you use your legs, push with your back, and give with your hands.

What to do if . . . *the horse canters too fast.*

You may be gripping with your legs to hold yourself in the saddle. If you close your legs, the horse goes faster, so don't start that boulder rolling. You must ride on balance. Don't grip.

An outside influence, such as cantering toward the barn or toward other horses, can also cause your horse to speed up. Change this by cantering away from such influences.

What to do if . . . *the bounce is uncontrollable and you can't sit down.*

You're probably tense and 180 degrees out of sync with the horse. You're going down as he's coming up. First, relax. This is supposed to be fun.

Observing more experienced riders can prove invaluable. You will naturally emulate their motions. Consider having yourself videotaped so you can see what you're doing wrong. Sit down and talk to your instructor. If you just aren't getting the hang of it, maybe now is the time for that private lesson or two.

What to do if . . . *the horse runs away in the ring.*

Usually the horse isn't actually running away, you're just having trouble stopping him. The first thing you must do is *listen,* even though this is really hard to do, especially if you're panicked. But listen. Your instructor will be telling you what to do.

Get your horse turned and circle him toward your instructor. Keep reducing the size of the circle until the instructor is in the center. At that point the horse will stop at the instructor or the instructor can stop the horse for you, or at least give you directions.

Canter Leads

As you advance your riding, you'll be asked to make sure your horse picks up the right lead. In other words, when Sampson canters on right rein, or clockwise, he leads the canter with his right front leg — it goes forward slightly more than the other front leg — and when he canters on left rein, he leads with his left. This helps his balance.

At this stage of cantering, however, I do not work on leads. It's just too much for you to absorb while you're still trying to find your canter seat. But this is something you need to be aware of and that you'll learn soon.

You're on track if you can:

- ✓ Control the horse and keep your half seat position as he picks up the canter.
- ✓ Maintain the half seat position comfortably for a full lap around the ring.
- ✓ Sit through a few strides of the canter without gripping or trying to stand in your stirrups.

How Do You Tell a Horse's Age?

Horses don't get wrinkles, crow's-feet, or double chins, but there's another way to tell their age: making an educated guess based on the appearance of their teeth. Although this is a very inexact science, it's often possible to come within five years or so of the horse's age.

The horse has plenty of teeth: 12 incisors in the front and 30 molars behind. The horse bites off grass with the incisors and chews food with the molars. The interdental space between these sets of teeth is where the bars are and the bit goes. Some horses grow "wolf teeth" in this space — pointy little teeth that usually come in on the upper jaw. Because they sometimes interfere with the bit, wolf teeth are often removed when the horse is young.

To age a horse, veterinarians look at the incisors. They look for evidence of wear on the lower teeth and for the appearance of a line, called Galvayne's groove, that forms from the gum line down in older horses on two of the upper incisors.

Trail Class

Trail Riding is without a doubt one of the most enjoyable riding experiences you can have. In teaching books, including this one, authors talk a lot about what might go wrong and how to fix it. But trail riding is actually relatively safe if you ride in a controlled situation. You get to relax, take in the peace and quiet of nature, and do it all from the back of a very good friend.

For this lesson I'm assuming you have an instructor leading the trail ride as part of a class, but I'll also include some information that pertains to trail riding in general.

A horse like Guinness will keep you on your toes on the trail.

Guinness

AGE: 15
WEIGHT: 1,100 lbs.
SIZE: 15.1 hands

BREED: Quarter Horse
COLOR: Sorrel with white
blaze and stockings

Guinness is named after the ale because of his personality. If he were a man, he'd be loafing on the sofa, sipping a Guinness, smoking a cigar, and watching Monday night football.

When he walks out of his stall, he unenthusiastically ambles along. Some days, you'll think he might not make it to the ring. But then every once in a while he'll surprise you with a burst of energy.

Guinness is an especially beautiful, traditionally bred Quarter Horse. Muscular and sleek, he has sturdy legs, a bold head, and the classic Quarter Horse butt, huge and powerful. Guinness, however, also happens to be a *cribber:* He has the bad habit of hooking his front teeth on his stall door and arching his neck. It sounds like he's sucking in wind. (See photos on page 82.)

Most of the time he's calm and steady, but like most horses, he'll shy at the unexpected. He also likes to snatch at grass and trees if given the opportunity, so you've got to be on your guard and let him know at all times who's in control.

Guinness makes no fuss about being led out of the barn, but when you cross the yard to the ring, he goes for the grass. Keep his head up. Let him know he's not going to pull this stunt on you.

a

b

▲
*A horse that hooks his front teeth on something and appears to suck in wind is called a cribber (**a**). A cribbing strap can help minimize cribbing (**b**).*

Cardiovascular Fitness

The exercises presented so far have focused on improving muscle strength and endurance, but this is only part of true fitness. Your cardiovascular system also needs to be maintained and strengthened. Walking several times a week, running, or using a treadmill or exercise bike are all excellent options. Do, however, get your physician's approval before beginning cardiovascular conditioning.

Preparation

Before you hit the trail, there's one minor thing you have to learn, and that's jumping. Trees might have fallen across the trail, and carrying a chain saw with you just isn't a good option.

Don't get too excited. You're only going to negotiate some poles on the ground and *cavalletti* (poles that have been raised a few inches). After that, it's off to try your skill at navigating ditches and logs.

Trotting Poles and Cavalletti

The key to riding over trotting poles and cavalletti is to keep Guinness going straight, get into half seat, and look up and beyond the poles to where you're headed. By getting into half seat before you reach the poles, you'll be secure when you feel the minor jolts as Guinness sails over these obstacles. Grab some mane, too, just for good luck.

Here you go. Trot Guinness straight over the poles. Feel the shock? Did you flex your joints and stay level on top of the horse while in half seat? If so, good! Go over the poles several times until you become comfortable with this exercise and can easily maintain your balance and your seat.

Now you're going to do the same thing over cavalletti raised three inches off the ground and then six inches. Guinness will start to jump a little, which will cause a little jostling for you! You must keep your body position by flexing your joints and staying level.

Logs

Next, try a real, live, dead log, which is just a little higher than the cavalletti. (Don't forget your half seat.) Guinness trots along

◄

Keep the horse moving forward when riding over cavalletti.

nicely, but when he comes to the log, what does he do? He hops. It was an awkward little jump. You lurch backward. Then you whip forward.

This is common. Some horses will walk or trot right over little poles or logs, but others hop or jump. Later, you'll learn more about how to encourage a horse to take a smooth little jump, but in the meantime, your half seat will help minimize the shock. Also, keep your reins short and hold onto Guinness's mane. A handful of mane will help counter that backward lurch. Otherwise, your whole body weight is going to pull on the reins and Guinness will get it hard in the mouth.

◄

Holding onto your horse's mane will help you maintain your balance as you go over logs in the field.

Ditches and Ravines

Horses tend not to like to step down into ditches or ravines, and Guinness is no exception. If it's a small ditch, he'll prefer to hop over it. Treat the ditch as if it were a log. Get into half seat and hold the mane.

Again, let me stress that you hold the mane and keep the reins short. If your reins get loose, you won't have the control you need if Guinness speeds up after hopping the ditch.

On the Trail

It's time to head out onto the trail. Other obstacles and things that could go wrong are hard to replicate at the barn. Besides, after all that riding in rings, you're probably anxious to tackle nature's course.

Natural Obstacles

You'll have to adjust your riding position a bit for the terrain. Guinness might also act a bit differently as he negotiates obstacles.

Hills

When climbing hills, keep your upper body in line with the trees. Most trees have enough sense to grow straight up from a hill, and you should emulate them while riding. If you were walking up this hill, you'd lean forward just a bit to stay straight. Do likewise when you ride.

So you reach the top of the hill and oops! Guinness speeds up! Don't panic. He's trying to get up onto level ground, where the going is easier. Use a half halt if he goes faster than you're comfortable with.

Warning: On a really steep hill, Guinness might even try to canter up. It's easier for him to get to the top if he's got momentum.

▶
When riding uphill, align your body with the trees.

Now go down a hill. Lean back just a bit to stay straight with the trees. (I think it's uncanny, by the way, how many of my students manage to find hills to go up, but ways to avoid coming down.) As the horse descends, he may speed up to reach level terrain. Or he may mosey down most of the hill, only to shoot out at the bottom. Half halt as necessary.

Water Crossings

Some horses, including Guinness, really hate to get their feet wet and muddy. Be forewarned. A tiny creek lies ahead.

The key to negotiating this obstacle is preparation. Get into half seat. Keep your reins short, and grab mane. What's Guinness going to do? He jumps it. But you were prepared, so you managed this little jump just fine.

Another, much wider stream lies ahead. Guinness can't possibly try to jump this, and he doesn't. What he does do, though, is stop to take a drink. Now he's playing, pawing the water with his feet. How funny, how sweet.

Alert! Get Guinness going and do it now. You're holding up the riders behind you. Not only that, but Guinness is thinking about taking a bath with you on him! He's pawing with his feet to splash his tummy so the cool water won't be such a shock when he rolls in it. So get Guinness moving through that stream or suffer the consequences.

Mud

Now you encounter a wide, muddy, shallow ditch. Guinness steps right in, but his feet start to sink. This muck is deeper than you realized. Guinness is sinking up to his fetlocks, and he's starting to panic. He thrashes a bit to get out and starts backing up.

You know that if he'd just get through this mud hole, the footing would be okay on the other side. But Guinness's survival instincts are kicking in and he wants to head for home. In this situation, let Guinness back out. Give to the horse. Then help him find a better crossing. He just might know more about this muddy ditch than you do.

If you encounter a muddy area where the horse doesn't sink much, treat it as water. Get into half seat, grab mane, and encourage Guinness to move on through to more secure footing.

Brush

You shouldn't be riding in heavy underbrush at this point. But if Guinness somehow manages to get his legs caught up in underbrush or branches from a fallen tree, and if he starts to act jittery about it, dismount. Do it immediately.

Make sure you take the reins over his head so you have more control from the ground, then allow Guinness to work his way out of this jam. You don't want to do this while sitting on his back, because he may have to go through some pretty violent gyrations to free himself. You and most other riders simply don't have the ability to ride this out. Horses, by the way, usually do manage to extricate themselves from such tangles.

Bees

While trotting along at a leisurely pace, you approach a low log. Guinness whacks the log with his hind feet, and bees start swarming. They're after the horse in front of you, Guinness, and the horse behind you.

The horses start jumping around a little bit and flinching. If your instinct is to try and run the horse away from the bees, don't do it. Bee stings are minor compared with hitting a tree. However, moving briskly away is certainly in order. But keep the ride tight. Make sure you have perfect control of your horse. If Guinness begins getting out of control or you feel like you're about to come unseated, let everyone know right away.

Suppose the swarm is really big, the bees attack fiercely, and all the horses in the ride start to act up. All riders should dismount and fend for themselves. You cannot, at this stage of riding, control a mounted horse that's getting stung by bees while you're also getting stung. It's better to dismount and escape the bees with your feet on the ground.

Branches

You've survived hills, water, mud, and bees on this trail ride. What else can happen?

You're moseying along and come to a part of the trail where the branches of some small trees have grown out at the rider's height. The rider in front of you grabs the branch and pushes it out in front of her as she passes. You prepare to do the same, and whack! The branch whips back and smacks you in the face.

Part of trail etiquette is not grabbing branches. You can use your hand to move them aside, or perhaps lift them up and over your head, but don't grab them and certainly don't turn them into whips that will smack the rider or horse behind you.

Briars

The trail narrows with a lot of underbrush protruding. Guinness suddenly lurches forward, as if he got goosed. Briars scratched him. Maintain a good posture, not a sloppy one, so you'll be ready for the unexpected.

Burrs

Guinness is acting panicked again, lurching forward periodically and tossing his head around. It's time to dismount. Your instructor will help you figure out what's wrong.

It's a burr stuck in his tail. Every time he swishes, he gets stuck in the butt again. The poor guy feels like he's whipping himself. Get out that burr as quickly as possible.

Overhanging Limbs

Beware! The 14.2-hand pony and the 5-foot rider on him made it under that tree limb up ahead. But your horse is 15.1 hands and you stand 6 feet 2 inches. You might not make it under that limb, so be prepared to duck.

First Aid

Some of the basics for a first-aid kit include rolls of gauze, gauze pads to stem bleeding, antiseptic, antibiotic ointment, adhesive bandages for abrasions and minor cuts, and those ready-to-use ice packs for strains and sprains.

Gaps and the Accordion Effect

Suppose you're fifth in the line of six riders. One instructor leads and another brings up the rear. The one in front controls the speed of the ride to keep the horses behind her from galloping off. She can block the path if need be.

An instructor also will often make it a point to ride a safe school horse herself so that if something goes wrong with a student's horse, she can switch mounts.

The third horse in line starts to trot. Soon, the fourth also begins to trot, and suddenly a space opens up in front of you. What does Guinness do? He starts cantering. He feels left behind and wants to catch up. Now the fourth horse hears him coming, and he begins cantering, and before you know it, the entire trail ride is cantering. This is not a good situation.

You can prevent this from happening by keeping a steady pace. Don't let a gap develop between Guinness and the preceding horse. Stay about one horse length apart.

Communication among riders, particularly about changes in gait, will also help prevent gaps. Pay attention. If, for instance, your instructor says, "Let's trot," follow through. If everyone adopts the same gait and pace, gaps don't form.

Unfortunately, there's usually one rider in every crowd who wants to make the ride more exciting, so he purposely hangs back so his horse will canter to catch up. Your instructor is trying to keep you safe, so listen to her. You'll have plenty of riding excitement soon enough.

Shying

You're riding along peacefully, enjoying the scenery, and suddenly a deer jumps out of the woods on the right. Guinness dips and spins to the left. He just shied. Shying, or spooking, means that something, either real or imagined, scared the horse or that the horse is just playing around.

Sudden movements often will cause a horse to shy. So will unnatural or misplaced objects. (I've never figured out why people haul refrigerators into the woods, but they do.) Old balloons, pieces of paper, and plastic bags are other things that might set off a horse. So will shapes that do not blend into the background, such as a jagged, blackened stump at the edge of a green field. When you see something that doesn't blend in, be ready.

Horses move away from whatever scares them. If something scares Guinness from the rear, he'll move forward — right into the horse in front of you, if he's frantic enough. If the scary thing comes at him from the left, he'll move to the right.

To handle a horse that shies, stay relaxed, sit down in the saddle, and keep a low center of gravity. Maintain your posture. Do not lean forward or back. Keep your feet under your hips and your shoulders down. The lower your center of gravity, the better.

Your reins have a lot to do with staying on a horse when he shies. If your horse shies to the right, you're at risk for coming off the left side. To counteract this, push both hands toward what made him shy. In this instance, you'd bring both hands to the left side of the horse. You'd also put weight in your left stirrup and your right hand.

This accomplishes two things. First, since your momentum is to the left when the horse shies right, you're supporting yourself in a way that will help center you in the saddle. Second, shying to the right bends the horse left and by putting pressure into your right hand and supporting your weight on the right rein, you're straightening him and bringing him back underneath you.

In my opinion, there is no such thing as a horse that will not shy. You can have the calmest, most dependable horse imaginable, but something out there will still be capable of frightening him. This is why you never want to take what I call a sloppy posture. You must always be prepared.

What to do if . . . your horse becomes a runaway while on the trail.

This might happen if you're riding home toward the barn and you somehow manage to get in front of your instructor. This is a big no-no, but suppose it happens.

Forget about all the movies you've seen where the knight in shining armor rides up, grabs the reins, and stops the horse. It ain't gonna happen. In a horse race, the chances of anyone grabbing another horse's reins is slim indeed.

Your best option is to use a pulley rein. Hopefully, your instructor will be close enough to talk you through. If not, you're on your own. If possible, turn your horse onto another path.

If that's not possible, you *must* use a pulley rein. Remember, it's like trying to start the lawn mower. The quicker you can jerk the reins, the better your chances of regaining control. If you have to jerk more than once, keep the reins taut enough between jerks to prevent your horse from pulling out farther and faster.

Too often in runaway situations, riders initially think they can handle things, but too often they are wrong. If you let your horse stretch out like a race horse, he'll just get more out of control. Stop him, and do it now! Do it as harshly as you need to.

The Emergency Dismount: Pro and Con

Almost every certifying agency for instructors teaches a maneuver called the emergency dismount. I disagree with teaching it to students.

I've seen more students hurt practicing this move than I've ever had injured in normal riding. You're supposed to practice the emergency dismount at the trot, the goal being to vault off the horse and land on both feet. This is supposed to prepare you to dismount if a horse takes off at a gallop and you can't stop him or if you're headed for danger.

But it just doesn't work that way. I've seen students suffer broken arms and ankles because they didn't land correctly while practicing. In addition, when the horse sees you jumping off out of the corner of his eye, his instinct may be to strike out with a hind leg.

Once you've slowed a runaway down to a slow trot or walk, go ahead and dismount if you want to. But I do not recommend trying to jump off a horse that's trotting fast, cantering, or galloping.

This is my viewpoint, based on my experience. Other people may disagree, so listen to your instructor.

What to do if . . . the entire group of horses is out of control.

This is a more serious situation than a single runaway. Each horse's behavior is feeding the others' behavior. Separate the horses, if possible. Turn yours in a different direction — down another path or into a field you pass. There's another important riding rule to learn here: *Never fight a runaway horse on a straight line.* So get your mount turned and follow the same procedure as for the individual runaway.

Etiquette

Trail riding etiquette is important for all riders' safety, comfort, and pleasure. It can mean the difference between a good riding experience and a bad one.

Stopping, Dismounting

You're trotting along again nicely on the trail, and suddenly you feel nature calling. "Instructor, can we stop so I can go to the bathroom?"

Avoid getting yourself in this situation. You might find it difficult to remount on the terrain, or your horse (or the other students' horses) might get antsy and try to head for home while you're on the ground.

The only reason to dismount in a class trail ride is to deal with an emergency or to make a tack adjustment. And you should've checked your tack carefully before you even left the barn.

Never fight a runaway horse on a straight line. Turn him if you can.

Right of Way

The class has ventured onto multipurpose trails. Hikers and bicyclists also use them. Because you're on a big animal that can move quickly, you yield. It's the polite thing to do.

To yield the right of way, always back your horse off the trail at an oblique angle. His head should face into the trail, with his butt directed toward the woods.

Trespassing

You've come upon a field marked "No Trespassing." The field looks as if it would provide a wonderful ride. You bet the owner wouldn't mind if the class took a little jaunt across the property. After all, you're not hunting or riding off-road vehicles.

If it doesn't belong to you, if it's posted, if there are crops planted, if it's a turf farm or a putting green, you can bet you don't belong there.

Bad behavior by horseback riders contributes to antihorse sentiments. It just works against you in the long run. So respect the property of others, and especially "No Trespassing" signs.

The Return Trip

You're finally headed home after an exhilarating ride on the trail. You've jumped logs, forged streams, and cantered up hills. As you reach the halfway point, Guinness may begin acting more energetic and walking faster.

Hurrying Back to the Barn

Half halt frequently and be especially careful not to let big gaps form between you and the preceding rider. In general, the ride should be tighter on the way home.

If Guinness persists in walking faster than you want in his rush to get back to the barn, remember never to fight him on a straight line. Turn him left for four or five strides, then right for four or five more. Repeat as necessary. If the trail is so narrow that you haven't got enough room to work him left and right, keep his head just off center. If you don't, here's what will happen. As Guinness gradually speeds up, he'll push his nose out to the front and take an inverted posture. The snaffle bit will no longer work. You might as well be riding him with only the cheek pieces. By turning his head to the side, he can't evade as much.

Darkness

The instructor meant to take a short trail ride and get you home before dark, but with everyone having so much fun out in the woods, time has flown by and the sun's going down. Don't worry, because Guinness can see much better at night than you can. Trust him to take you home, and just be careful not to bang your head on an overhanging tree limb.

If you find yourself at a point where you think you should go left but your horse thinks you should go right, go right. Chances are your horse is correct, especially if you're headed toward the barn. (Otherwise, trust your instincts.)

Getting Lost

You won't get lost if you trust your horse. Mind you, Guinness might graze all the way and take hours to get there, but he'll eventually get you home. No question.

You're on track if you can:

- ✓ Take the half seat position and stay steady in the saddle while negotiating poles, logs, ditches, and water holes.
- ✓ Maintain proper spacing on the trail.
- ✓ Ride responsibly, both to protect your safety and the safety of others, and to respect other people's rights and property.
- ✓ Keep your head and act appropriately when the unexpected happens.

Getting Help on the Trail

Carrying a cellular phone on the trail is a smart thing to do, and I'd recommend that all instructors taking out trail rides carry one. It's the best way to get help.

If no one has a cellular phone and a rider gets hurt badly enough that she or he can't ride or walk, then whomever is the most well versed in first aid should stay with the injured person. The rider that can ride the fastest and the most safely should head to the barn for help. The other riders also should turn back, at a steady, calm pace. The goal is to get help as fast as possible without endangering anyone.

If you're the one going for help, make sure you know how to get back to the injured person; watch for trails with the closest access and for places where emergency personnel with a gurney can get through.

Whether on the trail or in the ring, do not walk your horse near anyone sitting or lying on the ground. If the person moves, your horse may shy, and being stepped on may mean further injuries. In general, keep the number of people around the injured person to a minimum. Use basic, sound first-aid procedures.

Perfecting the Canter

ALL OF THE THINGS you've learned so far in this book come together in this lesson. You've been working hard to establish your seat. Once you've done that and also learned to reasonably collect your horse between your hands and your legs, you'll be far more able to control the horse, and you'll find the canter very comfortable.

Your horse for this lesson is a special one.

Justin

AGE: 12
WEIGHT: 1,100 lbs.
SIZE: 15.1 hands

BREED: Morgan
COLOR: Dark bay with
  a stripe

Justin is regal and gorgeous. He knows it, too, striking a pose as if to say, "Just look at how great I am. I'm above all the ordinary school horses in this field." He prefers Red Delicious apples and will turn up his nose at a sour Granny Smith any day of the week. He even rolls in mud elegantly. Justin has one little problem. He overreaches, that is, his back feet hit his front heels, so he has to wear ***bell boots*** to protect his front feet.

Justin isn't a full-blooded ***Morgan***. He's a mutt. That's just as well, because many Morgans can be a bit more than a beginning rider can handle. Whatever other breed Justin has in him has made him a good, well-rounded school horse.

Justin's also very smart. We're talking brilliant. He waits for you to give him the aids, and they'd better be clear directions. He wants you to be the leader and will test you to see if you can meet his standards. Think ahead with this horse. If you panic and grip, Justin won't stop, he'll move on and out.

Breakdown of the Aids

To prepare for your cantering lesson, you should begin by reviewing the aids to the canter. Like all gaits, the canter requires that you position your body in various ways to get the horse to move as you want. To make this easier, let me break down the aids to the canter so they really make sense.

Aids to the Canter

Preparation

1. **Half halt.** You give a half halt to let the horse rebalance and know you're going to tell him to do something different.
2. **Pick a point.** This is a physical spot on the ground. It's an inch. It's a centimeter. It's *very specific*, because to initiate the canter the horse has to change the way he moves, and so do you. If you don't time this correctly, Justin may run into the canter (trot faster), or he may have a delayed reaction to the canter, which could unseat you.
3. **Sit down.** You have to sit fully down in the saddle because the horse is going to gather his body underneath you and change how he's moving, and you need to follow with your back.

Bending the Horse

4. **Position your legs.** Position your inside leg at the girth and your outside leg behind the girth. (Remember, "girth" in this context refers to where you sit in proper balance, directly on your seat bones.) At this point, you just position your legs, which remain passive.
5. **Position your hands.** Shorten your inside rein, but both reins should still have equal contact with the horse's mouth. What does this mean? You're turning the horse's head to the inside, but because the contact remains equal he doesn't turn his body. (Of course, if you pulled on just the inside rein, he'd turn). This establishes a bend, which will help Justin pick up the correct lead. More on that later.

Execution

6. **Squeeze with your outside leg.** You actually squeeze with both legs, but make your outside leg the active one.
7. **Push with your back.** Do you recall the swing analogy from way back in lesson 1? Imagine sitting on a swing with your feet off the ground. You want the swing to move forward, so you push forward with your back.
8. **Give with your hands.** I don't mean throw your reins away. I mean release the pressure that your leg and back have created.

The sequence of the aids is critical. The motion must be initiated from the rear toward the front: legs, back, hands.

The Correct Lead

You need to understand leads. In the canter one front foot — the leading foot — steps farther forward than the other. *If Justin is on the correct lead, then his inside front leg strides farther than his outside leg as he canters.*

Mind you, there are rear leads, and horses can be on one lead in the front and one in back. If this happens you'll recognize it, because your body will feel like it's being thrown in four directions at once. This is called **cross-cantering**, or a disunited canter.

The lead relates to the horse's balance. What determines which lead the horse takes is the bend in his body at the exact *second* that he begins to canter. That you bent him beforehand doesn't count. What matters is that he has the correct bend precisely when you pick up the canter.

▶

At the canter, the horse's inside front leg should stride farther than the outside front leg.

Recognizing the Correct Lead

How, then, can you recognize the correct lead? The first way to tell — I don't recommend this, but everyone does it — is to lean over the horse's inside shoulder and watch his feet hit the ground. But be aware that you could run into the fence or, if Justin suddenly stops, fly off over his shoulder.

A better alternative is to look down at his shoulder points. Notice that with his front legs extended at the canter, both shoulder points are forward, but one is farther ahead than the other. This should happen whenever your seat has dropped fully down and is about to start on its back stroke.

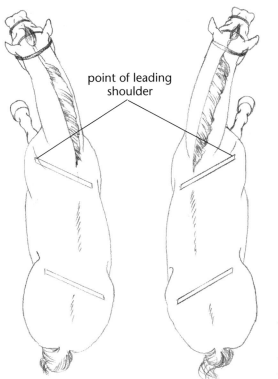

point of leading shoulder

Upper Back Strengthener

This upper back postural exercise will help you maintain a more upright position in the saddle.

Stand up and raise your arms to the side at about shoulder height. Bend your elbows 90 degrees so your hands face forward. Move your arms backward so your elbows come toward each other. Hold for about three seconds, and then release. Be sure to keep your arms at shoulder height so you work your upper back. Repeat about five times initially, more if it's comfortable for you.

◄

A more advanced way to identify the correct lead is to observe the position of the horse's shoulder points. The inside shoulder should be farther forward than the outside shoulder.

There's another, even better way to confirm a correct lead. When you canter on the correct lead, your outside hip will turn to the inside. If, however, your inside hip turns toward the outside, you're on the incorrect lead. When you can distinguish these differences in how your hips move, you're starting to learn to really feel the horse — a definite indication of your progress. As you get even more skilled at the walk, trot, and canter, you'll be able to recognize when a particular hind foot hits the ground.

Observing Others

The very best way to identify the correct lead is to observe more advanced riders cantering their horses. Watch as they pick up the correct lead. Before you know it, you'll be able to pick out the correct lead readily.

The Incorrect Lead

There are many reasons why a horse will pick up the incorrect lead. First, horses have preferred sides, just as people are left- or right-handed. Correctly trained horses are reasonably ambidextrous but can still show a preference for one side or the other. Justin, for example, prefers the right lead, and he'll pick it up much more easily than he will the left, although he can do either if given proper direction.

Also consider the possibility that you bent the horse improperly or gave the aids to canter incorrectly. Justin has to know which way he's going. Sometimes, he makes an assumption and picks up that lead. Say, for instance, that while cantering down the center of the ring Justin assumes that you'll ask him to turn right when you reach the fence. Then you give him ambiguous or incorrect aids. He picks up the right lead even though you meant for him to go left and to pick up the left lead.

Stiffness, not being ambidextrous, can also cause a horse to pick up the wrong lead. Some horses will only canter on one lead because that side of their body is overdeveloped. My students often ask why this happens. Suppose you brush your teeth with your right hand all the time. If you were to break that hand and had to brush with your left hand, wouldn't it feel foreign and uncomfortable?

Finally, an incorrect lead may result simply because a horse is still a horse. Given the choice of turning toward or away from the barn, he'll turn toward the barn. Don't underestimate such outside influences.

Recognizing the Incorrect Lead

You should recognize after the first stride or two if your horse is on the incorrect lead. Watch for the following clues:
- He doesn't canter exactly when you say — there's a stutter step. He probably changed his bend during that step and assumed the incorrect lead.
- He raises his head and becomes inverted during the transition from trot to canter.
- He trots faster or, in other words, was strung out during the transition.
- He usually is very balanced on the right lead, but you're going left.

Fine Tuning

Now that you've perfected getting into the canter with your horse on the correct lead, you have to figure out what your body is doing and how to control it. Remember, you're riding on balance, not gripping. If you grip, you won't be able to do any of the things I'm now going to describe to you.

Your Seat

When you initially start to canter, your seat will slide back and forth on the saddle, sometimes generating enough friction to toast your buns. This won't happen if you keep your seat bones in place, in the saddle, while following Justin's motion. You accomplish this by collapsing and straightening your spinal column, particularly from the bottom of the rib cage to the bottom of the seat bones. When the saddle drops, collapse; when the saddle comes up, straighten.

This resembles rolling your hips at the sitting trot, but with more of a twisting action. On a turn, your outside hip will go farther ahead than the inside hip. At all times, keep your body relaxed.

Perfecting your canter seat will take you fully five hours of practice at the canter. If you have a chance to practice alone, be careful not to overdo it. Don't unwittingly abuse your horse. You may want to learn so badly that you keep cantering and cantering, which can fatigue a horse. Show a little compassion. Give your mount plenty of breaks and variety.

Breathe!

While learning to canter, don't forget that your body needs oxygen. When most students learn to canter, they hold their breath, which often explains why they can't seem to go more than once around the ring. Breathing is good for you. So breathe!

Your Hands

If you watch a horse canter, you'll notice that his head moves up and down. But it also moves forward and backward, and your hands have to follow this motion. Of course, as your horse becomes more collected at the canter the movement will decrease, but in the meantime you must learn to follow it.

Hold your reins between thumb and forefinger. Having your hands in the proper position will give you the flexibility in your fingers and wrists to follow this motion. Otherwise, you absorb the motion at your elbow, which causes a distinct flopping of your arms.

Controlling the Speed of the Canter

Most beginning students have trouble learning to control their seat and their hands simply because the horse is cantering too fast. Their hands and legs flop, which tells the horse to go faster, causing more flopping, and so forth. You have to break this cycle, which means getting your horse to canter slowly so you can learn your position.

As the leading foreleg strides forward, try to restrict how far it extends. This means that as your seat comes down, you pull back. I hate to use the word "pull," but that's what it is. What makes this pull work is the *release* — relaxing the pull during the recovery stride — before reapplying it to the leading foreleg. One of the principal rules of riding comes into play here: *Steady pulls on a horse will not work.*

Next, you must bend your horse during a turn. If you lean on a turn when riding a bicycle, you go faster. If you lean when riding a horse, he'll accelerate just like the bicycle. To maintain a slow canter, you must keep yourself and the horse upright, and to do that, you'll have to bend him to the degree of the turn.

As always, the secret to controlling a horse is anticipating his thoughts and correcting errors before they occur. If you're cantering merrily around the ring and you turn toward the barn, you can bet he'll canter faster. He might also speed up if he's trying to catch the horses ahead of him. Tell him with a half halt not to do that, before he gets to the corner.

A single half halt may be enough both to correct him and to signal him about the coming bend at the corner. You may, however, need an extra half halt.

To help you better understand the role of half halts here, try this. While practicing, begin a running conversation with the horse, telling him out loud what you want. You'll find yourself warning him not to do things; these are all half halt times. Sometimes your voice won't be sharp, and sometimes it will. Now use your hands, your back, and your legs, adjusting the intensity of the half halt as you did your voice.

Keeping Your Horse on Course

To steer your horse at the canter (or, for that matter, at any speed or gait), imagine taking him down an imaginary line. You don't want him to deviate off that line by more than a sixteenth of an inch. You accomplish this by looking up (most people incorrectly look down at the canter), focusing on where you want to go, and controlling Justin's thinking.

If you allow Justin to veer two feet off that imaginary line, it's almost impossible to recover without breaking stride or using extreme aids. Instead, sense nuances and make minute corrections. Keep your horse on course to begin with. The rein aids you learned at the trot also work very well at the canter.

What to do if . . . you can't pick up the correct lead.

Analyze why the horse or you are having difficulty and communicate with your instructor. The horse could be stiff. He might be trained to obey a different set of aids. In fact, some horses are trained to bend to the outside to pick up the correct inside lead. You have no way of knowing this without talking it over with your instructor.

What to do if . . . you bounce uncontrollably while cantering.

This usually results from standing up in the stirrups. If you don't allow yourself to come fully down into the saddle, a space forms between your seat bones and the saddle, you grip, and the gap gets bigger with each stride. The solution is to take a bounce, immediately collapse your spinal column, and then start to follow the horse.

If you bounce only on the turns, you're propping yourself with one leg or the other to counterbalance the leaning of the horse. So bend your horse and stop propping.

What to do if . . . your horse trots faster instead of cantering.

Your horse may simply be misbehaving, but you probably forgot to use the progression of aids or failed to build the contained energy needed to canter.

You're on track if you can:

✓ Pick up the correct lead at the canter four out of five times.
✓ Make smooth and precise transitions into the canter, without your horse tossing his head or otherwise resisting.
✓ Bend a cantering horse into a corner without leaning.
✓ Keep cantering on a 20-meter circle without breaking stride.

How Many Hearts Does a Horse Have?

Ask a horseman, and he'll tell you a horse has five hearts. There's the one in his chest, of course. But he also has four auxiliary pumps — one inside each hoof.

They're called plantar cushions, and each resembles a sponge. As the horse picks up his foot, the sponge fills up with blood. Putting his foot back down compresses the sponge, pushing the blood back up the leg.

Lesson 10

Training

Look at how far you've come. You just learned how to canter and now you're about to train horses. Not bad, huh? What you may not realize, however, is that you've actually been training horses since that very first lesson, when you rode Sprite. In fact, every time you sit on a horse you train him. The training may be good, bad, or indifferent, but that's what you do.

Now you need to learn more about the basics of training, including more about how the horse thinks. After this lesson, you'll be ready to advance your riding proficiency by leaps and bounds. (Nope, that's not a cliché: Lesson 11 introduces jumping.)

Your horse for this lesson is a **warmblood** named Max. Max isn't for rank beginners, but guess what? You're no longer a beginner. If you've mastered all the skills in the previous lessons, riding Max should be a real treat. Don't ever forget your basics, however, including safe leading procedures and checking that girth before you mount.

Max

AGE: 9
WEIGHT: 1,300 lbs.
SIZE: 16.2 hands

BREED: Hanoverian
COLOR: Dark bay,
    white star

Max has multiple personalities. He's either very, very good or very, very bad. I really do think he has a split personality. One moment, he's very sensitive to the leg, and the next minute, he's not.

In his stall, he's the biggest slob in the world. We have to pay stall muckers extra just to go in there. He also scatters his hay around and overturns his water buckets at every chance.

Amazingly, this slob has good ground manners. He's one of the more advanced, highly trained horses in the barn, and he's usually kind to riders, when he's in the mood.

A Horse's Mentality

Horses are intelligent, but only to a degree. To them, 2 plus 2 might be 22, but it never will be 4. You can't explain this to them. When it comes to riding, however, they're smarter than you. They'll amaze you with their ability to learn, as well as with their clever evasions. That's why training horses is rewarding, but challenging.

To train a horse successfully, you need to appreciate these governed principles of equine behavior:

- Horses are creatures of habit. Routines make them comfortable. That explains their tendency to head for the barn, where everything is familiar and routine.
- Survival is predicated upon flight. Horses run first and ask questions later.
- Horses are herbivores and instinctually eat almost continuously. Don't neglect their stomachs if you want to win their hearts.
- Because horses are gregarious, herd animals, expect them to respond as a herd.

◀

Horses are herd animals and are easily influenced by other horses.

Using Their Instincts

The easiest way to see how these principles, these instincts, come into play in training is to apply them to a training exercise. Suppose you want to teach a horse how to **leg yield**, that is, move laterally away from the pressure applied by a rider's leg.

Habit

To train a horse to leg yield, should you ask him to move toward or away from the barn? Obviously, you use his instincts by moving him toward the barn.

Should you ask him to leg yield in the same spot or at various places around the ring? In the same spot, of course, because horses are creatures of habit. Eventually you'll have to move to other places, but take advantage of his instincts when starting out.

Survival

On which side of a horse should you hold a crop? Because a horse's principal defense mechanism involves flight, he tends to move away from pressure. So if the horse is moving away from your left leg, hold the crop in your left hand.

Eating

Training an animal, whether a dog, a chimpanzee, or a horse, requires punishments (irritation, pressure, pain) and rewards. What's the greatest reward for a horse, other than your getting off his back? Food! You could literally train him to move away from your active leg every time a feed can rattled. Of course, that would be impractical, but now and then you can bend over from the saddle and give him a piece of carrot or maybe a peppermint (perhaps a little raw meat if you're riding Nemesis). Food can be a viable and valuable training aid.

Herding Instinct

As you teach a horse to leg yield, should you move him away from or toward a group of other horses? If possible, capitalize on his desire to be with the herd, and move him in that direction.

Adding Logical Sequences and Repetition

You train a horse not only by using his basic instincts, offering rewards and meting out punishments, but through repeating logical sequences that the horse can understand. This last factor is very important. Studies suggest that a horse may have the mentality of a two- or three-year-old child, but with a child you can communicate verbally, show by example, and even use pictures and videotapes. Imagine, however, trying to teach a three-year-old to tie his shoelaces only by manipulating his limbs. You might be able to do it, but it would take a long time and much hard work.

That's about what it takes to become a horse trainer — time and hard work. The only way you'll succeed is by using a horse's instincts, rewards and punishments, a logical sequence, and repetition, repetition, repetition.

The Corridor of Aids

The language for training is much more detailed than the language for riding. Training requires a "corridor of aids." Think of this corridor as having flexible walls and a door at the front and back.

- You control the front wall with your hands. To move the whole wall forward, you push with both hands. If you push with just one hand, the corresponding side of the front wall swings forward. If you pull back with both hands, the wall comes toward you.
- You control the back wall by working your seat in conjunction with your legs. If you close both legs, the back wall moves forward. If you press in with one leg, the corresponding side of the back wall moves forward. If you cease using both legs, the back wall falls away.
- You control each side wall through the legs, seat, and hands on that particular side. For example, if you close your right hand, press in with your right leg, and put weight on your right seat bone, the right wall moves in.

Example: Moving to the Left

Play with this corridor a little bit by asking Max to move directly to the left (a full pass). What do you do?

1. Close the front wall, because you don't want him to move forward.
2. Close the back wall, too, because you don't want him moving backwards.
3. Make the whole righthand side active, and open (make passive) the whole lefthand side.

What does this mean? Sit on your right seat bone, close your right leg at the girth, and hold the horse's head and neck straight with your hands. That will cause the right wall to move left. In other words, the horse will take a step to the left. Yes, this is a leg yield.

Of course, many things can go wrong. Max might walk or drift forward, back up, bend to the left or right, or just stand there. But with subtle and continuous adjustments of the corridor of aids, plus reinforcement, you'll accomplish this movement.

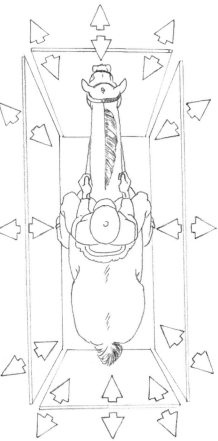

▲

Hand, leg, and seat aids can help you control a horse's movement in all directions. This idea is referred to as the corridor of aids.

Horse in a Box Frame

To use another analogy, when training horses think of each as being in an old-fashioned box frame. The frames come in all sizes and shapes. The frame a particular horse travels in is determined by the parameters you set through your legs, back, and hands. You never allow the horse to venture outside this frame. Horses that attempt to do so must be corrected.

Example: Moving Forward, Long and Low

Now try a longitudinal move. You want Max to move forward, long and low.

1. Push the front wall forward.
2. Close the back wall.
3. Keep both side walls in close so the horse stays straight.

To ask a horse to move forward, long and low using the corridor of aids, push the front wall forward, close the back wall, and close in on the sides.

What to do if . . . your horse evades by shifting his hindquarters to the left and traveling crookedly.

Close the left hind quadrant of the left wall. Bring your left leg back, behind the girth, position your right leg at the girth as a guard, and push the hindquarters to the right, back into the corridor. You're now traveling straight and forward.

Example: Marching Forward

Suppose you now want Max to march, that is, move with a more elevated step.

1. Close the front wall. Set it by pushing down your thumbs, but lift your hands to make sure it doesn't collapse.
2. Force the back wall up underneath the horse's hindquarters. Move both legs behind the girth with a slapping motion, and take a very deep, driving seat.

Max is jumping up and down inside the corridor. Make sense? Good! You're now a trainer. You know how and when to use your corridor of aids.

◀

To ask a horse to march forward using the corridor of aids, close the front wall and force the back wall up underneath the horse's hindquarters.

More Advanced Movements

You should now have enough preparation and confidence to learn a few *dressage* movements. These are exercises taught to a horse to develop his muscles, much as you'd use push-ups and chin-ups to build your biceps and triceps. If done correctly, these exercises build the right muscles; if not, they're worthless.

Here, however, the goal isn't to develop the horse's physique or prepare for a dressage show. Instead, I want to teach you how these exercises affect the horse's mind and movements and how you can use them to your advantage.

It's really not critical that you do the movements perfectly. The best way for you to get a feel for training is to experiment with a horse that already knows many of these specific movements — a horse like Max. You don't yet have the skill you need to actually teach a horse these movements. Trying them on an untrained horse would be a frustrating experience, even though the corridor of aids will work to some degree even then.

Leg Yielding

Leg yielding — moving Max laterally — can be done at the halt, the walk, or any other gait. Many other books describe in great detail how the movement should look and feel, but few describe the aids for a leg yield. Why? Because there are no aids specifically for this movement. Every horse responds differently to the leg and the subtle cues given by the rider. The following aids can, however, serve as a guide, despite the many adjustments you may need to make.

Assume you're traveling on left rein in the ring and want Max to leg yield to the outside. Come off the track 20 feet or so, enough to give yourself room to move back toward the track.

Aids to the Leg Yield

1. Bend the horse.
2. With the outside hand, use a leading rein.
3. With the inside hand, use a direct rein. (If the horse resists the progression, use an indirect rein behind the withers.)
4. Position the inside leg at the girth.
5. Position the outside leg passively behind the girth.
6. Keep the inside seat bone weighted.

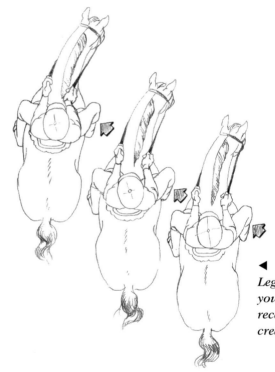

◀
Leg yielding is driven by your legs. Your hands only receive the energy you create with your legs.

Those are the aids. To execute the move, start driving with the inside leg and inside seat bone. You want Max to go forward and laterally. Your hands must receive the surplus energy you create with your legs and your seat, while your inside leg directs energy laterally.

Note: Most newer riders try to turn this leg yielding exercise into a hand yielding exercise. Leg yielding has nothing (almost) nothing to do with your hands.

You'll probably fail during your first attempt at the leg yield because either your hands don't receive enough energy or perhaps your legs haven't created enough energy. You must practice to find the point where the horse is between your hands and legs. There you can direct the horse's energy to execute the leg yield.

Turn on the Forehand

The turn on the forehand is the first basic movement that asks a horse to move without stepping forward or backward. Here, your legs impel direction independently of your hands, with Max's hindquarters revolving around his front end.

There's a perfect way to do each dressage movement, but don't worry about perfection; instead, I want you to concentrate on how Max moves away from your leg without forward motion. The turn on the forehand, by the book, requires the horse to turn 180 degrees by crossing the hind legs while remaining straight. One foreleg, the pivot, marks time in the same spot. The accompanying illustration should help you understand. What you're doing is changing the rein, but without bending or moving forward or backward.

You accomplish this through the corridor of aids:

Aids for Turning on the Forehand

1. Set your hands. Remember, your hands control the front wall. You don't want your horse to go forward, so you set your hands.

2. Apply seat and legs. You want to close the back wall so the horse doesn't back up. Since he can't move forward or backward, his instinct will be to move left or right.

3. To turn the horse clockwise, apply both legs, but with your right leg behind the girth. The horse will move his hindquarters away from this pressure.

Repeat this set of aids for each subsequent step, making any necessary adjustments. Keep doing this until Max has rotated 180 degrees and you're now on the right rein.

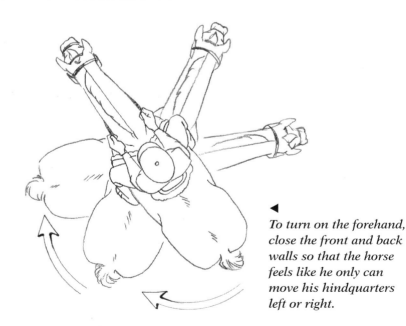

◄

To turn on the forehand, close the front and back walls so that the horse feels like he only can move his hindquarters left or right.

Shoulder In

The shoulder in movement asks you to bend the horse while moving straight ahead. Although designed to develop muscles, this exercise also helps the rider and horse with canter leads, since picking up the correct canter lead requires the horse to bend.

To execute the shoulder in, the horse's front and hind legs cross, with the right front and left hind lined up — assuming you are on left rein. The horse bends just enough so that you can see the outside corner of his eye. But at the same time, his direction of travel is straight.

Practicing this movement will improve your understanding of how the degrees of intensity that you apply relate directly to the balance between your legs and hands.

Aids to the Shoulder In

1. Position the inside leg at the girth.
2. Position the outside leg behind the girth.
3. Keep the inside rein active.
4. Keep the outside rein steady, or supporting your inside leg.
5. Keep your hips or seat turned to the bend.
6. Keep the inside seat bone weighted and active.
7. Position your shoulders and head toward where you're going.

Half Pass

The *half pass* is a little more complex than the preceding dressage exercises. With a half pass, you move forward and on a diagonal, typically at 45 degrees. One front leg crosses the other and one hind leg crosses the other.

Unlike a simple leg yield, the horse, ideally, bends in the direction you're traveling. In a half pass to the left, the horse bends left. However, this is very difficult to do. Few horses have been trained to this level. If you can achieve a half pass with the horse straight, good enough.

In summary, the corridor of aids should bend the horse at the same time that he moves forward on a diagonal.

Aids to the Half Pass (to the Left)

1. Position your right leg behind the girth, keeping it active.
2. Position your inside leg at the girth.
3. Keep your left hand closed slightly more than your outside hand, just enough to create the bend. (The major tension will be in the right hand, just as your right leg will be your most active leg.)
4. Sit on your left seat bone.

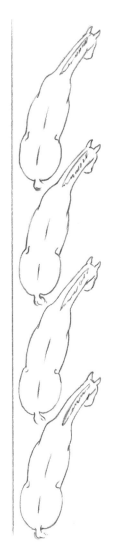

▲

The shoulder in command asks the horse to move forward and bend at the same time.

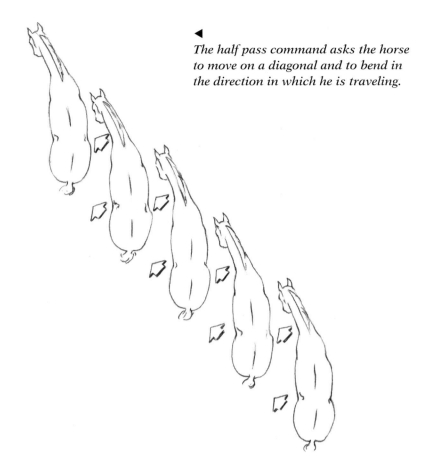

The half pass command asks the horse to move on a diagonal and to bend in the direction in which he is traveling.

Full Pass

Performing a full pass requires the horse to move directly to the side with no bend, crossing both the front and hind legs. This movement is very complex, but it will help you understand contained energy and how to displace it.

Where can Max go? To the open side, or the left wall. You have to achieve a fine balance among the various aids here to get Max to perform this exercise. A lot will depend on how each horse is trained in response to certain stimuli.

Aids to the Full Pass (to the Left)

1. Close the front wall.
2. Close the right wall.
3. Keep the back wall closed.

When performing the full pass, the horse remains straight (no bend) and moves sideways crossing both front and back legs.

What to do if . . . you can't perform an exercise.

In almost all instances, you haven't balanced the aids correctly. Say that when you ask your horse for a turn on the forehand, he just walks forward instead of revolving around the pivot foreleg. Your front wall isn't holding and the horse is walking through your hands. Fix your hands and your front wall.

Or suppose your horse walks around the circle instead of revolving. In this instance, you probably have a bend and perhaps your seat is at fault, too. Somewhere a wall isn't holding fast or the balance of intensities is off.

You're on track if you can:

✓ Reasonably execute a leg yield (to a corner).
✓ Perform four strides of shoulder in.
✓ Execute a turn on the forehand.
✓ Complete a half pass, staying straight (or even with a slight bend).
✓ Execute a full pass — four steps! Pretty good!

The Basics of Training a Horse

In essence, to train a horse, you must be able to do the following, not perfectly, but with a measure of skill:

- **With your hands:** turn the horse's head either way, slow him down or speed him up, and control the frame he travels in.

- **With your legs:** drive your horse forward, elevate him, or elongate him, plus move him laterally or bend him, depending on leg position and intensity.

- **With your seat:** restrict motion, encourage motion, facilitate lateral movement and bends.

No, you can't master all this in 10 lessons. Give yourself time. For now, focus on learning the corridor of aids as soon as possible. And don't foget that the horse must be reasonably trained for you to attempt dressage movements.

ONWARD AND UPWARD

PART 3

Jumping 101

I**T'S TIME TO JUMP**, folks! Realize that if left on their own, horses will walk a half a mile out of their way to avoid a simple 1½-foot jump. To get them to jump, you've got to do your part.

Jumping probably began long ago because horses were a primary means of transportation, and to get from here to there, they had to be able to negotiate obstacles. Today, we will jump for the pure fun of it.

But you do not *have* to jump. In fact, many of my adult students don't jump. They stick to dressage and other types of riding that require no jumping. Those who do jump, however, find it challenging and exciting. Moreover, many equestrian competitions require jumping to some degree.

In teaching you to jump, I'm going to proceed much as I did with cantering: one phase at a time. But first, make sure you feel comfortable negotiating trotting poles and cavalletti as well as jumping from the trot, which you learned during your trail class. If you don't, keep practicing those basic maneuvers and postpone this lesson.

For your introduction to jumping class, I've lined up an exciting mount for you.

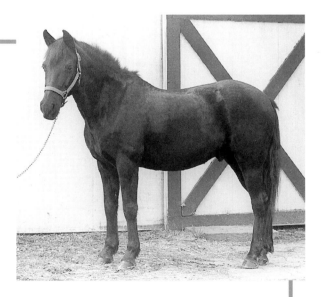

Magic

AGE: 8   BREED: Pony mutt
WEIGHT: 850 lbs.   COLOR: Dark bay
SIZE: 14.1 hands

A compact, almost black, attractive little pony, Magic was gelded late in life and still thinks he's a *stallion*. He just loves the girls. He neighs hard and prances around his stall anytime a mare walks by, and he'll try to get amorous if he's turned out to pasture with a mare. He'll also try to fight with horses three times his size. He's so aggressive around other horses, in fact, that he has to be turned out alone.

For riders, Magic provides a lively mount. He's fast, agile, and a fantastic jumper despite his size, which is why I've assigned him to you for this lesson.

Since you're riding Magic, I'm going to tell you the truth about ponies. Yes, they're certainly cute, and some people consider them smarter than horses. Contrary to popular belief, however, being small does not make them nicer. In fact, many of them can be difficult to handle.

You've already read that Magic acts up around other horses in the field, which means you should keep him away from other horses when you're riding. If he can get into a scrap, he will. Apart from that, you'll find him well behaved, and he'll give you a great ride.

Jumping Safety

In learning to jump, your chances of falling off your horse triple. You must protect yourself. Follow these very important rules:

- Wear a jumping vest. I highly recommend them, just in case you take a spill. They help protect your torso; some have pads that also protect your shoulders.
- A correctly fitted, ASTM/SEI–approved helmet is a *must!* You can no longer borrow some ill-fitting helmet.
- Don't jump if empty cups remain in the **jumping standards** (the upright or vertical end poles). The cups, which hold the horizontal poles you jump, are often made of metal. If you fall off and hit one, it could leave an ugly injury.
- Never jump a jump you aren't comfortable with. Expect your heart to beat a little faster while you're learning to jump, but don't let anyone force you into a jump you feel is too high.

▲
A jumping vest and helmet can help protect you if you fall.

Stirrup Length

For jumping, you want your stirrups shorter than usual. Your crotch has to be able to clear the front of the saddle, and your joints will be better able to absorb the shock of the landing after the jump.

To check your stirrup length for jumping, stand up in the saddle at the halt. With your heels down, your crotch should clear the front of the saddle by about two inches.

The First Jump

You're going to start with cross rails, which is an X jump, formed by crossing two poles. Magic's actual height off the ground during the jump will be about 18 inches.

Some instructors don't like to use this type of jump for beginners. If the approach isn't dead center, or the horse jumps either left or right of center, the height may be too much for some new jumpers.

My theory is that using an X jump teaches students and horses to aim for the exact center of the jump. In fact, I use X jumps almost exclusively for teaching beginners. Students not only find them less intimidating than other types of jumps, but ultimately realize the horse is actually jumping higher than the center of the X, which can build a beginner's confidence.

But this is my way; you should start out with whatever jump your instructor deems best.

▶

This is an X jump made from cross rails. The standards are the upright end poles; the horizontal poles rest on cups. If the horse hits the poles, they will readily fall down. Illustrations of more types of jumps appear at the end of the lesson.

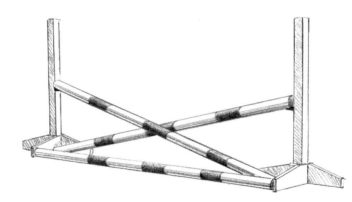

The Jumping Approach

Here's what you need to do to try your first jump:

Aids to Approaching a Jump

1. Travel at the canter in half seat.
2. Collect your horse.
3. Position your heels lower than your toes.
4. Look up at where you're going.
5. Arch your back slightly.
6. Hold onto the mane with the thumb and forefinger of one or both hands while keeping the reins short enough to steer.
7. Position your hands *two-thirds of the way up the horse's neck, underneath your forehead.*

At the canter, your heels drop down with each successive stride. You'll feel a definite lock between your upper calves and the horse. If you don't feel this, turn your toes slightly out to make sure you keep your legs on the horse. Keep your feet directly under your center of gravity.

A rider in proper position for approaching a jump will be in half seat, have her heels lower than her toes, arch her back slightly, and look where she's going.

A Note to Your Instructor

You might be wondering why I want the student holding onto the mane. Because this is a small jump, the horse won't extend very far over the jump; there's no crest release necessary (see page 116). Crest release will come into play once the horse starts **basculing**, or arcing over the top of the jump. Holding onto the mane helps keep beginners a bit more secure until they get used to jumping.

Stay Straight

You must aim Magic straight for the center of the jump. Don't approach it from an angle. When you jump from an angle, you make the jump twice as wide. The bigger the jump, the harder it can be to stay mounted.

Straight also means the horse should not bend, either to the left or the right. Look straight ahead. You should see neither of the horse's eyes as you approach. The jump should be in front of you, between Magic's ears.

Go Forward

The stride of a school horse is about 10 to 12 feet. Beginning three strides before the jump, you must go progressively faster, or forward, toward the jump. In other words, each of Magic's last three strides before the jump must have more impulsion.

*You must **crescendo** into the jump. Never slow down into a jump.* If you do, Magic will have to work harder to jump the jump. Instead of having forward momentum helping him jump in a graceful arc, he'll have to jump less smoothly and with greater effort, which may make it harder for you to stay on. The worst-case scenario is when a horse approaches a jump, stops completely, and then jumps.

The first, most basic rule is that you must go *forward* over the jump.

To make jumping feel safer, newer riders tend to slow down their horses as they approach the jump. But that's one of the worst things you can do. The horse has to use more effort to get over the jump, or he might stop completely before jumping. Both ways makes it harder for you to stay on, so go forward. Onward and upward!

Taking Off

Magic readies himself to take the jump by gathering his body in the following way:

- His front feet strike the ground for the last time, and with a push of his shoulders he raises the front of his body to the angle required by the jump.
- His hind legs come underneath him farther than normal, causing his back to round.
- He pushes off simultaneously with his hind feet, although one will be farther ahead, or leading.

When Magic pushes off, you must be moving forward, too. Staying still or standing up is not what you want to do, because if you aren't connected to Magic through your lower legs he'll literally jump out from underneath you.

If you get left behind, so to speak, you'll be forced to regain your balance. Unfortunately, poor Magic will catch your full body weight in his mouth because you're attached to it with the reins. This is why I recommend that you hold onto the mane until you get proficient at following a horse over a jump.

As your horse pushes for the takeoff, rise out of the saddle, following your horse's motion.
▼

As Magic's hind legs push, you need to close your lower legs (not your heels) to get the degree of the horse's effort required for the jump. When Magic makes this push, you come lower into the saddle, but as the push is extended you actually rise out of the saddle, following the horse.

As your jumping progresses to where you no longer need to hold onto the mane, you'll have to do a ***crest release*** during the jump. This means you move your hands forward, following the crest of his neck; you do this to the degree necessary to maintain steady contact with his mouth, while at the same time allowing him the freedom he needs to extend his body and neck for the fluid arc over the jump.

Over the Jump

I've said you should look at where you're going. But I've found that as beginning students go over the jump, virtually all of them look down, or even back, to see the jump. Don't make this mistake. It rounds your back and sets up a myriad of problems. Primarily, you won't be able to absorb the shock of the landing as well.

As you go over the jump, Magic will rotate slightly downward. Your upper body must rise slightly, but in no instance should you stand up.

▲
Approach: To tackle a jump, travel at the center in half seat.

▲
Takeoff: Crescendo into the jump.

▲
Over the jump: Close your lower legs and rise out of the saddle to follow the horse.

▲
Landing: Keep your eyes forward and back straight.

▲
Follow through: Travel straight for the follow through.

Building a Stronger Back and Hips

Here's another back-strengthening, hip-stretching exercise. Lie on your stomach. Bring your hands together and rest your forehead on them. Slowly lift one leg off the floor about two inches, hold for two or three seconds, and then lower it. Switch legs and repeat. Start slowly, and increase the number of repetitions gradually.

Landing

Magic is now angled slightly downward, with his front legs ready to land. As soon as this happens, Magic will push his head and neck up, and his hindquarters will drop down. If you're following his motion, your joints should easily absorb the shock when he lands.

The hindquarters will come under the horse farther than normal. In fact, they'll land very close to his front legs. To regain his balance, Magic has to push off with his hind legs again which will help him raise his front end off the ground. To encourage this recovery push, close your upper calves (again, not your heels). This is another place where you could get left behind.

Follow-Through

The jump is not over until the second stride after the jump. The follow-through upon landing is extremely important. To follow through, make sure Magic's pace doesn't change. He should not slow down. He must stay straight. Failure to follow through will sour a horse on jumping and make it extremely difficult to jump a course of fences, as you'll be doing in the next lesson.

During his recovery stride, don't balance yourself by pulling on Magic's reins. After the recovery stride, travel straight for at least two or three additional strides. It helps you and the horse regain balance.

What to do if . . . your horse stops in front of a jump.

The first and nastiest type of refusal occurs when the horse canters toward the jump, slams on his brakes, and doesn't jump. This is called, not surprisingly, stopping in front of a jump, or *quitting*.

▶

Your lack of confidence or a nearby distraction can cause a horse to stop in front of a jump.

Several things can cause quitting. Your horse's strides may have been mistimed for the jump, though that's not usually the case. More likely, during the approach the horse may have lost his confidence about jumping. Maybe your own lack of confidence played a part, or maybe something caught the horse's eye. Also, some horses simply fear jumping.

The most likely explanation, because it's a common problem among riders new to jumping, is that you slowed down on the approach. You may also have done something inadvertently that interrupted the horse's thought process during the approach.

Of course, try to ride so that your horse doesn't refuse a jump. But in case he does, make sure that you don't keep going when the horse stops. Keep your heels down. Look up.

What to do if . . . your horse ducks out to either side of the jump.

This can happen if your approach to the jump isn't straight, you're riding timidly, and/or you're communicating that you really don't want to take this jump at all. Rethink, reapproach, try again.

What to do if . . . your horse isn't crescendoing toward the jump.

All of the above reasons for stopping in front of a jump may apply. Incorrect striding, a lack of confidence on the part of the rider or the horse, or a poor approach can cause a horse to stop in front of a jump.

Dealing with Refusals

After a horse refuses, for whatever reason, you must turn him 90 degrees *away from the jump,* go back three or four strides, trot your next approach, and jump him immediately. You can't meander about getting him back into the jump. If it's a confidence problem, it must be dealt with directly. Take my word for it; I've watched literally thousands of refusals.

If your horse veers out to the left, you must turn him back to the right; reapproach the jump from the same side as before, and try him again. The farther you get away from the jump, the less likely you'll succeed on your second try. On the second approach, be sure to avoid a bend. Keep him going straight and forward.

▲
A horse may duck to the side of a jump if your approach to the jump isn't straight.

If a horse refuses to the left, turn him back right and approach the jump again.
▼

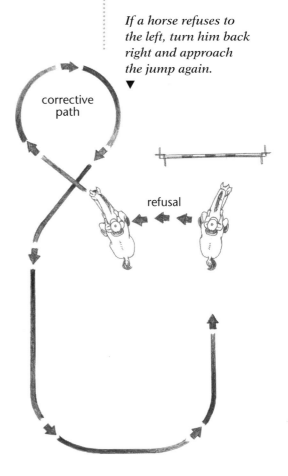

corrective path

refusal

What to do if . . . your horse pops, or chips, the jump.

Popping, or **chipping** occurs when the horse gets too close to the jump before actually jumping. It forces him to jump almost straight up and then come straight back down; he has no forward momentum to carry him up and over. Both horse and rider have to absorb the resultant shock.

All the reasons stated above for refusals can cause a horse to pop a jump, but the most likely cause is a striding problem. At this stage in your riding, the best way to avoid this is to be sure to go progressively faster the last three strides before the jump. You'll learn more on placing the horse for jumps in the next lesson.

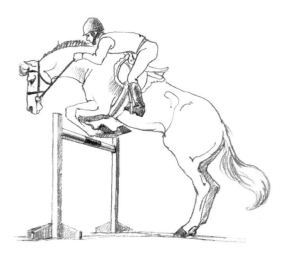

► *Incorrect striding is the most common cause of popping a jump.*

What to do if . . . your horse lunges toward the jump or takes off too far away from the jump.

If your horse takes off too early and lunges toward the jump, you may be left behind. Possible contributing factors include the horse's stride, his lack of confidence, or his overeagerness.

Remember that your horse must be reasonably collected coming into the jump so he has enough energy to release in the last three strides before the jump. If he's flattened out and not collected, lunging will occur.

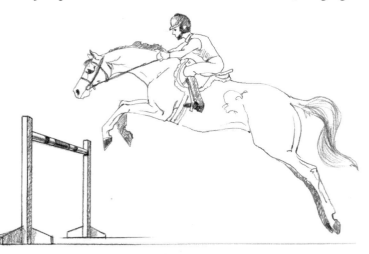

► *Overeagerness can cause a horse to lunge toward a jump.*

What to do if . . . your horse rushes the jump.

If your horse, through eagerness or fear, goes very fast toward the jump, he generally ends up inverted. A horse that does this usually takes the jump fast and flat, as in a steeplechase, where riders jump for speed over fairly flexible objects, such as hedges. But you aren't jumping for speed, and the poles you jump are comparatively inflexible.

The most logical way to fix this problem is to take a shorter approach. Another possibility is that your horse has become too keen on jumping and may require some reschooling.

◄

Take a shorter approach if your horse is rushing a jump and becoming inverted.

What to do if . . . your horse turns immediately after the jump.

This can be very disconcerting. Usually, it happens when a horse gets too used to jumping in a patterned sequence and anticipates the next jump. Try varying where you go after each jump.

What to do if . . . your horse hits or nicks the jump with his feet.

The timing — yours or the horse's — may have been off, or maybe one of you misjudged the jump in some way. By far, the most common cause of this problem is your catching the horse in the mouth or bouncing on his back.

In the case of misjudgment, you probably asked for too big or too flat a jump, since horses rarely misjudge height. You might have caused this by slowing him down before the jump or not making sure he had enough impulsion to go over the jump.

Also consider the possibility that the horse has jumped too much; he could be tired, bored, or just plain lazy.

You're on track if you can:

✓ Know when the horse is going to jump (so you don't get left behind).
✓ Jump the jump and stay mounted.
✓ Stay straight and keep your position throughout the entire jump.

Approaching Different Types of Jumps

Once you've mastered jumping the cross poles, or X jump, you'll want to try some other types. I'm going to describe how the horse will normally jump an obstacle and tell you a little bit about what can go wrong and how to approach each type of jump.

Vertical

When jumping *verticals* under about 2 feet 3 inches, you won't have much trouble if you follow the instructions detailed throughout this lesson. Once you exceed that height, however, it's not uncommon for a horse to try crawling up underneath the jump. In other words, his front feet wind up too close to the jump to jump smoothly. It's also called chipping in. A horse that jumps a vertical this way will break stride and jump in a very steep arc, at the risk of dragging a rail with his hind feet.

To jump a vertical, then, try to set your horse *back off* the jump — move your take-off spot farther back than where your horse would prefer. (More about the takeoff spot appears in lesson 12.) This should make the jump more fluid and more comfortable, even though the horse's instinct isn't to jump it this way.

When I say "set your horse back," I don't mean you should change his speed. What I mean is that well before those last three strides, adjust the horse's frame and thus his stride. Be sure you don't pull back on the reins in the last three strides, or you'll be setting yourself up for a refusal.

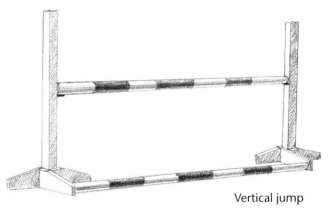

Vertical jump

Oxer

The *oxer* is really two verticals set close together. Although it can be intimidating for new riders, it's actually the easiest type of jump. The height usually matches the depth, and horses seem to prefer this.

Horses often jump an oxer in an almost classic, perfect jump, tracing a smooth arch over the top.

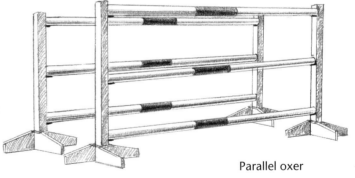

Parallel oxer

Hog Back

A *hog back* features a middle element that is higher than two outside elements. Horses usually jump this with too much arc. They may look down into the jump, or the back element may be difficult to see from the takeoff.

The best way to approach a hog back is to treat it somewhat like a vertical. Stand the horse back off the jump.

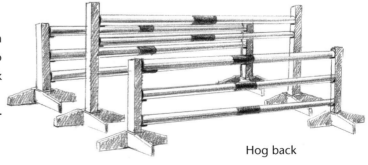

Hog back

Spreads

Spreads usually entail three or four elements. The height of the barriers and the depth of the spread determine its difficulty as well as how you approach and jump. The greater the depth, the longer and lower you want to jump. The greater the height, the more bascule (arc) you want.

What should you do if you confront a very high and very wide spread? At this stage of riding, avoid it.

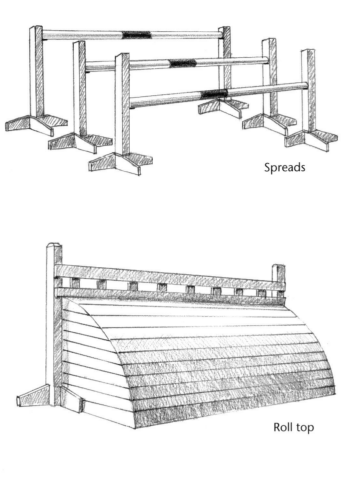

Spreads

Roll Tops

Horses tend not to like *roll tops,* though I'm not sure why. This is a solid, curved jump. It's not uncommon to see a horse get too close before jumping and then jump very high with no extension.

To counteract this, make sure you go aggressively forward toward a roll top.

Roll top

Diagonal Jumps

Diagonal jumps have one end higher than the other. Jumping competitions include them for one primary reason: They can set you off course, and there lies the challenge.

The design of the jump naturally leads you to one side or the other. The horse thinks it's a great idea to jump the low side of the jump, which will invariably put you in trouble for the next jump on the course. I guarantee that if you encounter a diagonal jump in a competition, jumping the low spot won't be to your advantage.

Jump the exact center unless you have a good reason to deviate — for example, because you can't set up for your next jump without clearing the higher end. While you're learning to take this jump, however, go for the center.

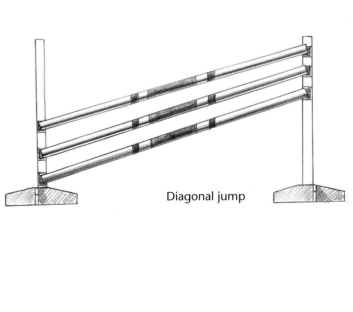

Diagonal jump

Lesson 12

Jumping 102

This FINAL LESSON covers two types of jumping: stadium (show jumping) and cross-country. The first involves negotiating a series of jumps in a ring or arena. It requires a lot of thought and planning. Jumping a course of fences can be scary, exhausting, and exhilarating, all within 30 seconds.

If you think that sounds thrilling, wait until you try cross-country jumping, negotiating jumps in open fields and in the woods. This is as close as riding gets to heaven.

And guess which horse you ride for this lesson? Good old Nemesis, that horse you met and rightly rejected in lesson 2.

Nemesis

AGE: 7 years old
WEIGHT: 1,200 lbs.
SIZE: 17 hands (get out the ladder)

BREED: Appaloosa
COLOR: Appaloosa is a color and a breed, too!
SEX: Gelding

Very tall, sleek, and muscular, Nemesis can be wild, bossy, and a real bully in the field. He tries to keep other horses away from the hay bale if he's eating and the water trough if he's drinking.

In his stall, he doesn't much like people disturbing him, especially at dinner time. If anyone walks by, he makes ugly faces. He sticks his head over the stall door, lays back his ears, shows his teeth, and waves his head. He consistently acts up when being shown for sale, which is why he's never been sold and why you're about to ride him.

Once he's tacked up, though, Nemesis's behavior generally improves, although he's been known to issue a nip if his girth is cranked up too tight, too fast. Under saddle, he's considered frisky. He'll also act up if the rider doesn't let him know who's boss or gets too confident too soon and doesn't stay on guard.

I'll bet he doesn't seem so intimidating anymore, does he? Once you're up on Nemesis, he's probably going to feel a lot like Tiki did in lesson 3. He moves ahead easily. This horse definitely has places to go and things to do.

Stadium Jumping

Generally, a stadium course has 12 jumps, but it can vary anywhere from 8 to 16. There are all types of jumps and configurations that require you to change direction and your horse's lead.

I'm not going to deal with competition, because the subject could take up an entire book. There are lots of rules and you have to learn about such things as scoring and penalties. But quite apart from the competitive aspects, you should know how to jump a course properly.

▲
A typical arena setup for stadium jumping will have several types of jumps.

Have a Plan

To jump a course of fences successfully, you must have a plan. Otherwise, all you'll be able to do is scramble through and hope for the best. In planning, remember to allot time for:

- Breathing
- Rebalancing
- Turns
- Course checks, or checking to make sure you're still on the correct course. Every third or fourth jump plant an imaginary flag to help keep you on course.

Breaking Down the Course

The biggest mistake people make jumping a course of fences is thinking of it as one long course. Instead, break the course down into a series of three or four jumps, and think of each series as separate. Usually, that gives you a beginning, a middle, and an end to plan out. Each has its own set of problems:

- The beginning — the challenge here is for you to get your horse going and for both of you to become comfortable with the surroundings.
- The middle — here you usually have to negotiate higher jumps and more turns; this requires a more technical approach to riding.
- The end — you're getting tired and may lose concentration, and your horse is getting excited and probably wants to speed up. You have to force yourself to focus and avoid rushing to the finish.

The height of a jump makes no difference. Course designers are quite capable of making an 18-inch jump practically impossible. For example, consider the difficulty of completing an 18-inch jump that's set at a 90-degree angle from an immediately preceding vertical of 3 feet, 6 inches.

The most difficult jump is the first one. I don't care if the first jump is 18 inches and the last jump is 6 feet. The first jump is still the most difficult because it's where you strive to establish the rhythm and attitude for the entire course.

The next most difficult jump is the last one. Now, the horse has no way to know which is the last jump. Only you know. But time and time again, I've seen riders inadvertently convey this to their horses either by letting down with relief or speeding up because they are excited they are almost finished. The horse ends up dragging off the last rail. If a course has 12 jumps, ride the twelfth as though there were 13.

Using Your Seat for More Control

In the previous lesson, you were jumping individual jumps. To jump a course of fences, you have to change how you jump. Jumping multiple jumps in different patterns and sequences and heights requires more control. Instead of just letting Nemesis jump the jump, as you let Magic do in the last lesson, you must take charge.

One way to get more control is by changing your seat. You need to sit in the saddle between the jumps rather than remain in half seat the whole time. But this should be a very light seat, not a full-balanced seat. Don't distribute all your weight on the seat bones; let your inner thighs support some of it.

This lighter seat will better enable you to make the transition from a sitting to a jumping position. In jumping a course of fences, you'll usually come from the sitting to jumping position at the precise second the horse pushes off with his hindquarters to jump the jump.

▲
Although you'll be in a half seat (above) while going over a jump, you may want to change to a light balanced seat between jumps for more control.

You can also use your seat to control Nemesis on the approach to the jump. For some jumps you'll sit on the approach, and for others you'll be up. Strive to become proficient at changing from a deep seat to a half seat.

Suppose Nemesis tries to slow down in front of the jump. Take a deep driving seat and drive him forward to the jump. Conversely, if Nemesis is keen and trying to rush the jump, take a light half seat, sitting on your thighs as opposed to your seat bones. When going over the jump, however, you should always be in the jumping position.

If this sounds tough, it isn't. In fact, by now you'll probably find that it comes pretty naturally.

Pace

Riding a course of fences involves pace and path. Pace is the more important of the two. Most people go too fast in a course of fences, on a horse that isn't adequately collected. The horse should be agile, his back rounded, and his hindquarters up underneath, helping to carry the additional weight of the rider. Keep his top line rounded, with his head positioned to receive direct communication from you with a minimum of resistance.

Your pace should be so steady on a course of fences that you can count each time the horse's leading foreleg rhythmically hits the ground. One of the most valuable exercises I teach is counting the strides around a course of fences, not just the strides in front of a jump.

Many kinds of things can destroy the horse's rhythm, including these:

- Bending to the outside around the corner, or leaning into the corner — these are two very common reasons for destroying the pace of a course. In both instances, the horse will speed up or change his rhythm.
- Not knowing where you're going — there's nothing worse than uncertainty. Horses hate indecisive riders, especially when jumping. Know the course as well as you know the floor plan of your home. You cannot change your mind once you set out on the course.
- Cutting corners — use the full dimensions of the course to give you time to control minor infractions.
- Approaching improperly — the more excitable the horse, the shorter the approach; the more lethargic the horse, the longer the approach. This will tell you that on Nemesis, for example, you'd use a shorter approach. When riding a horse like Toby or Sampson, you'd use a longer approach.

Other things that will destroy the pace include insecurity in the horse or the rider. Your anxiety can cause the horse to change pace or become anxious himself. A good way to relax is to remember to breathe.

▶
Keeping a steady pace between jumps is key to jumping a course of fences.

Path

In planning your path around a stadium course, allow for centrifugal force. If you're trying to turn a turn, the horse usually will drift to the outside.

The barn or the out gate also affects your ride. Nemesis is more likely to increase speed when moving toward the barn or out gate, and to decrease speed in the other direction. He might even break stride. You've got to take this into account as you guide him through the course and make the necessary adjustments to keep his pace uniform.

Different jumps require different approaches, of course. A low, wide jump requires a flatter, faster "strung out" approach, as opposed to a higher, vertical jump, which requires a more collected, slower approach.

The course layout also affects your approach. What you need to do in preparation for the next jump largely determines the angle you jump at, the degree of collection, and so forth. Say you're about to take a jump that will require a hard turn to the right after landing. You'll need a more collected, energetic jump than you would if the next jump called for a straight-on approach.

Stride

Jumping courses generally are laid out to a 12-foot stride, but some course designers throw in 18- and 10-foot strides. To jump a course of fences successfully and negotiate different types of jumps, you must be able to lengthen and shorten your horse's stride.

To lengthen the stride, take a more driving seat — sit down more fully in the seat — and pulse your lower leg more steadily. Keep your hands relatively steady, if not giving. (With some horses, you have to give just a bit to get them to extend.) Think of it as trying to create a longer, lower horse, but not a faster one. The longer stride will make you feel as if you're going faster, but your horse's pace won't actually change.

To shorten the stride, you want the converse — an elevated, collected horse. This means you take a lighter seat and deliver a sharper, slapping motion with your legs. You also set your hands more firmly, raise them, or both, depending on the horse.

Rating the Horse to the Jump

Adjusting Nemesis's stride and putting him in the correct spot to take a jump is referred to as *rating the horse to the jump*. Before you can do this, you have to develop an eye for the jump. This means being able to judge instinctively where the horse will take off for the jump, based on the distance to the jump as well as on the horse's speed and impulsion.

One way to develop this eye is by counting the strides out loud. Strangely enough, most people sense when the count will be off — when the horse is definitely going to take off for the jump at the wrong place — but they can't tell as easily when the takeoff will be correct. Fortunately, it's more important to know when it's going to be wrong.

The sooner you know Nemesis isn't going to hit the right spot to take off, the sooner you can adjust. Beginners usually know about three strides before the jump; advanced students know about eight strides before. If you're really, really good, you'll know before you come around the corner.

When It's Wrong, Drive

You learned in the previous lesson that you must go forward to the jump. Take this lesson a bit further: If the horse is going to be off on his approach to the jump, *drive*. Drive the horse with everything you've got! Your horse is probably out of stride and he's going to have to put in a chip shot — an extra little step — or take the jump very long. It doesn't matter; to get yourself out of this mess, drive.

Lead Changes

A course of fences will require you to change leads. The recommended strategy is to make a flying lead change on the straight line, but it's hard to do. Instead, change leads at the preceding jump or just before making the turn to the next jump.

Changing a Lead during Takeoff

Say you're coming into a jump on left lead, but you need to change to right lead to take the next jump. You communicate this change of direction to Nemesis by establishing a bend while over the first jump.

If you were going straight over the jump, you'd close both legs and push both hands forward at the beginning of the release, when you take off. To communicate a lead change, however, bend Nemesis during this phase — not as you go over the jump, but *during the takeoff phase,* when he gathers and releases. It's important not to do this too early because you could end up with a run out or a refusal.

To initiate this bend during the gathering, use your bending aids. Use both legs, the inside leg at the girth and the outside leg behind the girth. The outside rein will be longer than the inside rein, but with equal contact.

Sounds familiar, doesn't it? This is a common way to communicate a change of direction and establish a lead change. Of course, you must also look at where you're going, and when you land, your body must be poised to receive and react to this bend.

▶

To change a lead over a jump, bend your horse on the takeoff.

Changing a Lead Before a Turn

In the heat of jumping a course of fences, it's sometimes difficult to land on the correct lead. If you fail to get the correct lead over the jump — in preparation for the next jump — you can change the lead as you turn toward that next jump.

At the apex of the turn — the deepest part of the turn — you must establish a period of suspension so that Nemesis can physically change the bend of his body and the way his feet are traveling. This occurs during a split second. There's a break of the canter stride into the trotting stride, just enough time for each foot to hit the ground once. You accomplish the lead change here the same way you do any canter lead. But the half halt is a bit more abrupt and up. Remember, failure to jump off the correct lead or take corners on the correct lead in a course of fences invites disaster.

Upgrade Your Riding Attire

When you start to take jumping seriously, riding attire can really make a difference. You'll be driving your heels down a lot with jumping, and if you're also going to ride cross-country, you'll have branches and briars at your legs.

Proper, tall riding boots will help keep your legs from getting pinched and poked and will give you a better base of support than will lesser boots.

You already should be wearing an approved riding helmet and a protective jumping vest.

Drifting

In a course of fences, centrifugal force can be a friend or your enemy. Because of it, a horse will rarely drift to the inside. As you come around a corner, Nemesis is more likely to drift away from the turn, not into it. When you're riding a course of fences, then, you always aim for the inside standard.

Even if Nemesis doesn't drift to the outside, it's a fairly easy job to leg yield him out to the center of the jump, but it's nearly impossible to leg yield a horse back to the center of the jump once he's drifted wide.

Recovery Zones

I mentioned above that you should set up recovery zones. These are like planned rest periods, where you and Nemesis can regather yourselves. Just how many recovery zones you establish will depend on the length of the course. Usually, you plan one after every three jumps. Try never to extend that to beyond five jumps.

Leg yielding will become integral to this. You leg yield deep into a corner (get as close to the fence as you can) to create space where you can regather yourself and your horse and review your plans for the next set of the course.

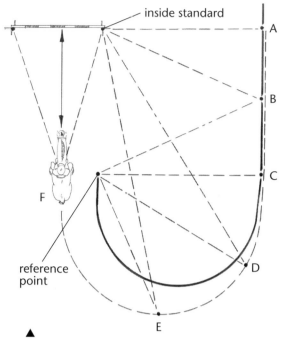

inside standard

A

B

C

D

E

F

reference
point

▲

A. *Parallel to the jump, look at the inside
standard.*

B. *Look at the inside standard, then at your
reference point (end of turn, in line with
inside standard).*

C. *Look at your reference point when you
are parallel to it.*

D. *Look at the inside standard, then at your
reference point.*

E. *At apex of corner, look at the inside
standard, then at your reference point.*

F. *No more than three strides away, you
should be heading toward the middle
of the jump.*

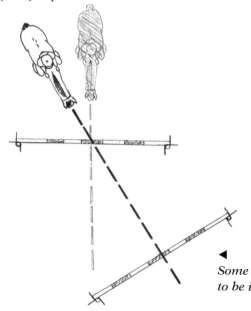

Approaches off a Corner

Your line of sight is very important. Four strides before the start of your turn toward the jump, you must look at the jump — more specifically, at the inside standard of the jump, not the jump in general. Then you look at the deepest part of the corner, where the turn is most acute, to begin gauging your approach to the jump. With each stride you now take, constantly check where you are, the deepest part of the corner, and the inside standard. Constantly. Once you reach the deepest part of the corner, focus on the remaining bend of the turn and on the exact approach spot for the jump.

This is of paramount importance before you start into a corner: Make sure your lead is correct! During this turn, it's critical that the horse stays equally balanced on all four feet, with his weight evenly distributed. He cannot lean into the corner. Complete your turn before you jump.

Jumping at an Angle

Some courses require you to jump at an angle to get the correct line for the next jump. Remember that doing so makes a jump wider for the horse. If at all possible, avoid jumping spreads, or any other jumps with depth, at an angle. This might include a water jump. The easiest jumps to take at an angle are verticals, although any angled jump will change how the horse jumps. Usually, he will jump bigger than you expect.

What to do if . . . something goes wrong within three strides of a jump.

Generally, if you are in the approach — within three strides of the jump — you have to jump the jump. Drive! Hard! Do not try to stop. Trying to stop a horse this close to the jump is a bad move. The horse could run out to the side or crash into the jump. Hold onto the mane and jump.

Let me make one exception. If the jump is 18 inches or less, you probably could stop the horse or turn him out without too much trouble. But when you get to higher jumps, the general rule is to drive the horse on.

◄

Some courses may require that you jump a fence at an angle in order to be in position to jump the next fence.

What to do if . . . you lose a stirrup.

This is not uncommon among riders just learning to negotiate a course of jumps, and it usually happens after a jump. Bring the horse down to a walk or trot and try to regain your stirrup; if you can't readily do so, stop before you enter the next approach and retrieve it. In a competition, you're never supposed to stop your horse completely, but while learning, always play it safe.

If you start losing one or both stirrups before the jump, it's usually because you're driving the horse forward and literally kicking the stirrup off your foot. To drive the horse forward, your legs should rotate back from your knee, not kick straight back. You also should be sure to keep your heels down. Lifting your leg can cause you to lose a stirrup.

What to do if . . . unexpected distractions occur.

Say you are *not* in the approach to a jump but something unexpected happens. A kite drifts over the course, or a motorcycle pulls up nearby. It might be something as mundane as another horse getting loose. Stop! Err on the side of safety while you're learning.

Otherwise, never give up, even if you ride the beginning of the course badly. Success hinges on your recovery times and continuing. Stop only for safety reasons.

Cross-Country

Jumping cross-country usually is done with speed, but it's a controlled speed. You can go as fast or as slow as you want within reason, traveling from jump to jump. But you must be in control when you face cross-country jumping obstacles.

One of the major challenges of cross-country jumping is the terrain. In the stadium, the ground is flat. In cross-country jumping, you might be jumping uphill or downhill. This adds a new dimension to your jumping experience.

▲
Cross-country jumping has its own set of challenges, including varying terrain.

Cross-Country Jumps

A cross-country course features natural (or man-made to look natural) jumps. They generally follow the same configurations as stadium jumps, but with a crucial difference: If your horse hits stadium obstacles, they fall down; if your horse hits cross-country obstacles, you fall. Cross-country obstacles are often fixed in place, like a big log.

Newer riders learning to jump cross-country often find that, when traveling with speed, they have trouble making a crescendo into the jump; they tend to jump flat. As a result, the horse bangs his legs — or worse, hangs up his legs — on the obstacles.

On the plus side, many horses actually seem to prefer cross-country obstacles to stadium jumps; I suppose because the obstacles are natural, horses tend to get along better with them. They also enjoy the freedom that cross-country offers.

Cross-country obstacles usually aren't high, with the degree of difficulty often being determined by the terrain before and after the jump. At this stage of riding, you won't be tackling water yet, but when you do, you'll find that jumps surrounded by water can be the most difficult.

Controlled Speed

Controlled speed is key to cross-country jumping. You should not still be riding with your thumb and forefinger in the mane. If you are, you're not ready for cross-country.

The jumping procedures are almost the same as for stadium jumping. However, in stadium jumping you can sit in the saddle to establish the control you need. In cross-country, it's a little more difficult because your horse is keener, moving along at a heady canter. Anything faster than that means you've lost control.

Try the following to maintain control while riding cross-country:
- Keep your reins short.
- Ride in half seat, a little more upright than for stadium jumping.
- Keep your horse straight.

Negotiating Terrain

All the principles for stadium jumping still apply, but the most important rule is to have your horse ***coming into hand***. When a horse is in hand, it means you have him in complete control. In fact, he comes so much into hand that the action almost seems like a pause executed six to seven strides before a cross-country jump. By executing an extreme half-halt, you can prepare to crescendo into the jump. Then you negotiate the obstacle much as you would a stadium obstacle, with the follow-through being extremely important.

Uphill Jumps

An uphill jump may be one of the easiest jumps you'll ever do, even though it looks intimidating during the approach. Horses prefer an uphill jump; it's easier for them.

You lose forward momentum on an uphill jump. Consequently, having your heels down and your upper calves locked into place is critical, and your upper body must be fully upright for the landing. *Look up!* Do not look down at the jump. To regather the horse, follow through and use a driving impulse on the recovery stride. If you don't, the horse might stumble.

An uphill jump looks intimidating, but it's actually one of the easiest jumps there is.
▼

Downhill Jumps

A downhill jump can scare cheese out of a milk cow, so prepare yourself. Keep your heels down and your upper calves locked in place. With your horse in hand, set your path during the jump and on the landing. The ground falls away from you and landing can feel like it takes an eternity. In the end, though, the landing probably will be smoother than you might think.

You naturally expect the horse to land on his front legs first, but on a downhill jump, all four legs hit the ground at about the same time. You may also find the downhill recovery stride disconcerting. Here, you need a lower posture and more collapsing of the joints to follow the horse's motion.

Hillside Jumps

When you take a jump on the side of a hill, you need to know what comes next; you must decide if you're going uphill, downhill, or forward after the jump. The horse invariably will choose downhill. But on every cross-country course I've ridden, the next jump is uphill.

Regardless of your path to the next jump, the best way to negotiate this obstacle is to jump so that the horse's front feet land as level as possible, not with one foot on higher ground than the other. This means jumping with the plane of the ground, probably at an angle. In effect, you're really turning this into an uphill or downhill jump.

Water Jumps

Don't go into the water. If it's a little puddle, jump it. If it's a larger water obstacle, don't do it. Water jumps require far more advanced riding skills than beginning riders have.

What to do if . . . your horse becomes crooked.

The horse wants to go faster, and you try to hold him back. To evade you, he bends. His hindquarters are no longer behind his front legs. He rotates his body weight onto his hind legs, much as he would when rearing, but without the rear. If he pushes off with both hind legs, as he would in a jump, his back and neck invert, your reins become ineffective, his mouth gets above the corridor of aids, and you risk traveling at terminal velocity.

Mind you, this happens over several strides. Your only protection is to recognize when it starts happening and correct the situation immediately, before it escalates. To do this, get the horse's hindquarters and

▲
For downhill jumps, be sure to keep your heels down and your calves locked in place.

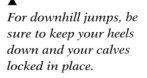

▲
If possible, make a hillside jump an uphill jump.

his front end directly in line however you can. Even if you have to kick the horse to get him straight, do it. If that fails, use a modified pulley rein or a pulley rein.

Even though leaning and careening around corners might sound like fun, it's not a good idea, especially in the woods.

What to do if . . . your horse becomes a runaway on a cross-country course.

Head up the hill, and use a pulley rein. But you should correct the problem before it happens.

What to do if . . . your horse stumbles.

Push with your arms into an upright posture or even get behind the vertical a bit, let your reins slide, and allow the horse to recover. Drive your heels down even to the point where your legs come in front of the girth.

What to do if . . . your horse suddenly goes lame.

Dismount. Check each foot for nails, sticks, glass, or anything else that might have punctured his foot. Remove it if possible before walking him back to the barn. If you can't remove such an object, seek help and do not attempt to walk the horse back.

You're on track if you can:

✓ Successfully count strides before a jump.
✓ Calculate takeoff points for different types of jumps.
✓ Do simple lead change while on course.
✓ Maintain a constant pace up and down hills.
✓ Recognize when the horse is crooked and fix the problem.
✓ Know when to start coming into hand for a jump (it's a lot farther back than most beginning jumpers think).

Appendix 1
Exercises

Tthe exercises suggested throughout the book are gathered here.
Remember, it's always a good idea to get your blood flowing and warm
up your muscles before doing any kind of exercise, including riding. So
take a walk around the block, run up and down a stairway, or jog in place.

The exercises presented below focus on improving muscle strength and
endurance, but this is only part of true fitness. Your cardiovascular system
also needs to be maintained and strengthened. Walking several times a
week, running, or using a treadmill or exercise bike are all excellent
options. Do, however, get your physician's approval before beginning any
physical conditioning.

Warm-up

The following stretches can be done after five minutes of aerobic activity,
just before class at the barn. To keep strain off your back, place your feet
hip-width apart, bend your knees slightly, and hold in your abdominal
muscles. Repeat each of the following four times before moving on to the
next, holding each move for a count of ten.

Reach way up over your head with both hands. Reach higher with the
left hand, then the right. With arms stretched out on either side, twist
gently left, then right. With hands on hips, bend sideways to the left, then
to the right. With hands on hips, bend forward from the waist, then backward as far as you comfortably can.

Calf Stretch

Stand on a step with the balls of your feet on the edge. Grab a hand rail
or balance yourself against a wall. Gently let your heels drop below the
balls of your feet, hold for two seconds, slowly lift up for two seconds,
and lower for two. Repeat five times initially. Do more as you're able.

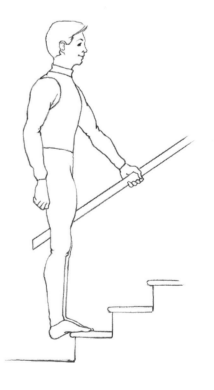

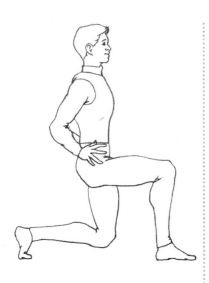

Modified Leg Lunge

Stand with your feet about shoulder width apart. Take one step forward with your right foot. Bend both knees until the left knee is about one foot off the floor, then slowly rise and bring the left leg forward. When bending, keep your knee even with or behind the toes of the forward foot. Repeat the exercise with your left foot forward. Do three repetitions on each leg at first and gradually build up.

Back and Abdominals Stregthener

Lie down on your back. Straighten one leg and bend the other at the knee. With elbows bent, put your hands behind your head and rest your fingers gently there. (Don't pull on your head.)

Tilt your pelvis so your lower back stays on the floor. Simultaneously lift your straight leg about eight inches and your upper body a few inches off the floor. Keep your elbows back, out of your peripheral vision, and your chin off your chest. Lower your upper body and foot to the floor simultaneously, lift up again, and then lie back. Repeat for the other leg.

This is a difficult type of sit-up, so only do a few repetitions the first time. Don't do it at all if it causes you pain anywhere. Gradually build up your stamina for this exercise.

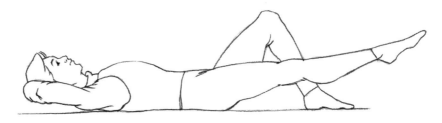

Inner Thigh Strengthener

Lie on your left side on the floor, with your left arm under your left ear and fully extended. Place your right hand on the floor in front of you. Bend your right knee until it also touches the floor in front of you. Lift your left foot (from the bottom leg), hold this position for three seconds, and then lower. Do two sets on each side. Increase the number of repetitions as you build stamina.

Hip Strengthener

Lie on the floor on your back with one knee bent and one leg straight.
Make a fist with each hand, and with palms facing down, slide fists under
your buttocks. (This protects your lower back and helps keep it on the
floor.) Your head also should remain on the floor.

Lift your straight leg as high as the top of the bent knee, and then
lower it. Now reverse your legs and repeat. Take it slow. Gradually build
up your strength. Do only a few repetitions at first.

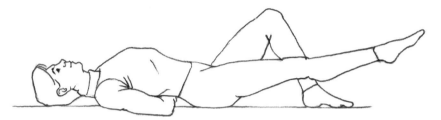

Quadriceps Strengthener

While standing with your hands on your
hips, place your feet hip width apart, your
toes facing forward.

Keeping your back straight and lifted,
slowly lower your buttocks behind you, as
if you were going to sit in a chair. If you
can, stretch your arms out in front of you.
If this is difficult, place your hands on
your hips or out to the sides. Slowly rise to
standing and repeat. Throughout the exercise keep your stomach muscles tight and
your weight in your heels. If you bend
straight down and don't sit backward
somewhat, it could create pressure on
your knees.

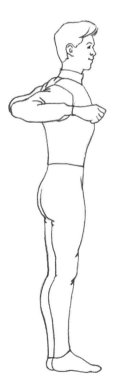

Upper Back Strengthener

Stand up and raise your arms to the side at about shoulder height. Bend
your elbows 90 degrees so your hands face forward. Move your arms backward so your elbows come toward each other. Hold for about three to five
seconds, and then release. Be sure to keep your arms at shoulder height so
you work your upper back. Repeat about five times initially, more if it's
comfortable for you.

Improving Balance

Get on all fours. Lift your left leg straight out behind you (not higher than your buttocks) and stretch your right arm straight out in front of you (level with your head). Take a deep breath, keeping your tummy tight. Hold for eight seconds. Repeat using the other leg and arm. Repeat exercise three times on each side.

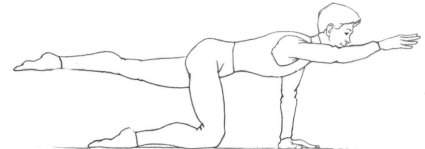

Building a Stronger Back and Hips

Lie on your stomach. Bring your hands together and rest your forehead on them. Slowly lift one leg off the floor about two inches, hold for two or three seconds, and then lower it. Switch legs and repeat. Start slowly, and increase the number of repetitions gradually.

Arm Strengthener

Get down on all fours, nice and square. With your knees under your hips and your hands below your shoulders, draw an imaginary line from the tip of one forefinger to the other. Drop your nose to the floor one inch in front of the imaginary line. Want to crank the intensity up a step? Drop your nose three inches in front of that line. Repeat three or four times at first; gradually build up the number you can do comfortably.

If you have bad wrists, you may not want to do this exercise or you may want to try it with your hands on a countertop instead of the floor.

Appendix 2
Standardized Aids

RULES OF RIDING

The sequence of the aids is important! Practice using them in the order given.

IN THE WORLD of English riding, we're lucky to have an organization called the Fédération Equestre Internationale (FEI) — the International Equestrian Federation. Headquartered in Switzerland, the FEI establishes rules and regulations for international equestrian sports, including the Olympic Games.

FEI also has developed standardized aids. Theoretically, if you go to Germany or France to ride English style, the horses will be trained to respond to the same, unadulterated aids. The use of standardized aids makes it easier for us all to learn, and certainly for instructors to teach. These are my interpretation of the FEI standardized aids.

Aids to the Walk

1. Sit down.
2. Squeeze with your legs.
3. Push with your back.
4. Give with your hands.

Aid to Add Impulsion to the Walk

1. Squeeze with your legs alternately (your left leg as your right hip comes forward, your right leg as your left hip comes forward).

Aids to the Halt

1. Sit down.
2. Set your hands.
3. Squeeze with your legs.
4. Push with your back into your hands.

Aids to the Trot

1. Sit down.
2. Squeeze with your legs.
3. Push with your back.
4. Give with your hands.

Aids to Add Impulsion to the Trot

1. Pulse (that is, squeeze and release) both legs simultaneously.
2. Drive with your hips.

Aids to the Canter

1. Sit down.
2. Position your inside leg at the girth.
3. Position your outside leg behind the girth.
4. Hold the inside rein shorter than the outside rein (but both with equal contact).
5. Squeeze with your outside leg (you actually squeeze with both legs, but make your outside leg the active one).
6. Push with your back.
7. Give with your hands.

Aids to Bend the Horse

1. Position your inside leg at the girth (this is your active leg).
2. Position your outside leg behind the girth.
3. Sit on your inside seat bone.
4. Turn your shoulders toward the bend and to the degree of bend.
5. Create the bend with your inside hand, giving equally with your outside hand.

Aids to Back Up the Horse (from the Halt)

1. Sit down.
2. Set your hands.
3. Squeeze with your legs.
4. Push with your back into and beyond the hands.

Glossary

Aids: Messages, or cues, you use to tell the horse what you want him to do.

American Cream Draft: A Draft Cross that's also a Palomino.

Appaloosa: A horse with white polka-dots, or spots.

Arabian: This is one of the oldest, most established breeds in the world, dating back thousands of years. Arabians have refined, elegant heads and large nostrils, and they carry their tails arched and high. They are used for many types of riding but especially excel at racing and long-distance riding.

Balance seat: Riding with suppleness, poise, and a judicious grip to preserve balance while on the horse.

Bars: The toothless part of the horse's jaw where the bit rests.

Bascule: The arc the horse makes as he goes over a jump.

Bay: Reddish brown or brown body with black points, which are the lower legs, mane, and tail.

Beat: When one or more of a horse's feet hit the ground.

Bell boots: When a horse overreaches, his back feet hit the heels of his front feet. To protect the front feet in such horses, bell boots are used.

Billets: Girth straps, attached to the girth of the saddle by buckles.

Bit: The metal mouthpiece that rests on the horse's bars and is used for control.

Black: A black horse is really black, all over, with no white markings.

Blaze: A wide swath of white on the face that runs from above the eyes to the nose.

Blue roan: A blue roan has a black and white coat with a bluish tinge.

Bridle: The bridle includes the headstall, which goes on the horse's head; the bit, the metal piece that goes into the horse's mouth; and the reins, which enable you to steer the horse.

Brown: A horse that is almost black, but not quite, or brown/black.

Canter: A three-beat gait. It's faster than a trot, and it is a natural gait.

Cantle: The back of the saddle.

Cavalletti: Poles raised off the ground, usually from three to six inches, that are used to help prepare horses and riders for jumping.

Check: A sharp, upward snapping motion with the reins.

Chip: What a horse does when he gets too close to a jump before actually jumping. Also called popping or chipping in.

Close: To pull gently on a rein, sometimes by simply closing your fingers.

Colic: Colic is a sign of abdominal pain, which in a horse can be caused by many things, such as overeating grain. A horse with colic will exhibit discomfort in many ways; he may paw, nod his head toward his middle, or thrash on the ground.

Collection: Asking the horse to assume a rounded, more agile posture.

Coming into hand: The horse is in your complete control.

Conformation: The horse's basic structure, or how the horse is "put together." The gait of a horse is determined by conformation. The more sloping the shoulders and pasterns, which generally should be the same angle, the smoother the ride.

Crescendo: A steady increase in intensity or force.

Crest release: Moving your hands forward, following the crest of the horse's neck, as he jumps.

Cribber: A horse that hooks his front teeth on something, usually the edge of his stall door, arches his neck, and appears to suck in wind. This is a bad habit some horses develop.

Crop: A riding stick, for use when leg aids don't get the desired response from the horse.

Cross-cantering: Also known as a disunited canter, this occurs when a horse is on one lead in the front and the opposite lead in the back.

Croup: The top of the horse's rump.

Dark bay: A very dark brown that's almost black.

Diagonal jump: A type of jump in which one end of the jumping pole is higher than the other.

Diagonals: Matching a trotting post to the horse's outside shoulder movement. When the horse's outside shoulder moves forward, the rider posts forward. When the inside shoulder moves forward, the rider sits.

Draft horse: Huge horses bred to pull heavy loads. They have a reputation for being calm and good natured, which accounts for why Drafts are known as "cold blooded."

Dressage: Dressage is a French word that means "schooling." Horses are trained to perform complex maneuvers by slight movements of the riders' hands, legs, and weight. Many riders worldwide compete in dressage competitions.

Drive: Forward impulsion.

English saddle: Style of saddle needed for riding disciplines such as dressage, jumping, fox hunting, and other equestrian activities.

Evasion: When a horse doesn't do what you ask or develops bad habits to avoid work.

Farrier: The person who trims hooves and shoes horses.

Gait: Way in which a horse moves forward.

Gelding: A castrated horse.

Girth: The strap that goes under the horse and connects to both sides of the saddle. However, girth can also mean where your legs fall when you're mounted and correctly balanced.

Give: To release the tension in the reins slightly.

Gray: Gray horses have white hair or white and black hairs on dark skin, with dark muzzles. There are many shades of gray, ranging from nearly white to very dark gray.

Half halt: Half of a halt, used to refocus a horse's attention or to signal that a new command is coming.

Half pass: A dressage movement in which a horse moves forward on a diagonal by crossing both front leg over front leg and hind leg over hind leg.

Half seat: A slightly forward sitting posture in which you flex your back, knees, and ankles to absorb shock.

Halt: A stop.

Halter: A halter goes on the horse's head and is used with a lead rope to control the horse while you're on the ground. Most are made of leather or nylon.

Hands: Horses are measured in hands, from the ground to the highest point of the withers. One hand equals 4 inches; a horse 14.2 hands high is 58 inches tall. Horses 14.2 hands and smaller are considered ponies.

Hanoverian: A Hanoverian is a type of warmblood developed in the eighteenth century. The breed is very popular in Germany. Generally somewhat heavier than other types of warmbloods, they are especially strong in the shoulders and quarters.

Hard-mouth: Said of a horse whose mouth nerves have been dulled, requiring a lot of pressure to get her to do what you want. It results from improper riding, training, use of too harsh a bit, or all of the above.

Hog back: A type of jump consisting of three elements, with the middle one higher than the outside ones.

Impulsion: Forward energy. A person marching has a lot of impulsion compared to when walking normally.

Jog: The trot, to Western riders.

Jumping standards: The upright or vertical poles with a base on them; they have holes in them where jumping cups can be attached. The jumping cups are where the jumping poles rest.

Left rein: Obviously, this refers to the left rein. But if your instructor says to you, "Trot out left rein," it means you should trot counterclockwise. The left rein is thus on the inside of the circle.

Leg yield: When a horse moves laterally away from the pressure applied by a rider's leg.

Mare: A female horse more than three years old.

Morgan: Morgans are an especially elegant and attractive breed with smaller ears, a nicely crested neck, and sloping shoulders. Many have a long, full, black mane and tail. Compact and powerful, with a sleek and noble appearance, the breed evolved from a stallion named Figure that was bred by a schoolmaster in Vermont named Justin Morgan. Morgans excel in a variety of sports; they are used for driving, pulling, and riding.

Mounting block: A box or stepping stool that makes it easier to reach the stirrup and mount the horse.

Near side: Always the left side of the horse.

Off side: Always the right side of the horse.

On the bit: See **Collection**.

Oxer: A type of jump consisting of two vertical elements set close together, with the height usually matching the depth.

Palomino: A horse ranging in color from pale cream to the color of a gold coin. The Palomino has a very light mane and tail, with few dark hairs mixed in.

Pommel: The raised area at the top front of a saddle.

Pop: See **Chip**.

Post: To rhythmically lift out of your seat with the movement of the horse.

Progression of the aids: The process of applying an aid or aids in ascending order of severity and with progressive intensity until a horse responds as you wish.

Pulse: To squeeze and release with both legs simultaneously.

Quarter Horse: The most popular breed in the United States and bred initially on the East Coast, Quarter Horses are thought to have originated from crossing Thoroughbreds with wild Mustangs. They were bred for acceleration power, enabling them to race a quarter mile. Many school horses are Quarter Horses.

Quitting: A horse stopping in front of a jump.

Rating the horse to the jump: Adjusting the horse's stride and putting him in the correct spot to take a jump.

Rising to the trot: Also know as posting to the trot. See **Post**.

Roll top: A jump in a half-round shape.

Set: To position your hands in one spot and apply steady, even pressure on the bit with both reins, but without pulling back.

Sorrel: A chestnut-colored, or reddish-brown, horse.

Spread: A single jump consisting of, typically, three or four barriers.

Stallion: An uncastrated male horse.

Star: A white diamond shape on the forehead.

Stirrup: Part of a saddle that hangs from the stirrup bar and provides a place for you to put your feet.

Stirrup bar: The metal piece under the saddle flap to which the stirrup leather is attached.

Stirrup iron: Part of a stirrup on which you place your feet.

Stirrup leather: Part of a stirrup that connects the stirrup to the saddle.

Stockings: White marks that extend above the fetlock, but not above the knee.

Strawberry roan: Also known as a roaned chestnut, this horse has a chestnut base coat and a sprinkling of white hairs.

Stride: When all four feet have hit the ground once.

Stripe: A thin white marking on the face that runs from forehead to muzzle.

Thoroughbred: Perhaps the most common breed of horse in the world, Thoroughbreds are best known for their speed and elegance. Most horses on the race track are Thoroughbreds, although the breed also excels in jumping and dressage. Because they are generally peppy and feistier than other horses, such as drafts, they are considered "hot blooded."

Trim: Hooves continuously grow and routinely need trimming by a farrier, typically about every eight weeks. In warm months, however, when the hooves grow faster, trimming every four to six weeks might be necessary.

Trot: A two-beat gait, usually faster than a walk and slower than a canter.

Two-point seat: See **Half seat**.

Vertical: A simple, vertical jump.

Warmblood: Generically speaking, any horse that's a cross between a cold-blooded (docile) and hot-blooded (feisty) horse would be a warmblood. But there's also a breed of horse known as the Warmblood. They have been carefully developed to produce a horse for competitive use. Types include the Dutch Warmblood, the Swedish Warmblood, and the Trakehner.

Western saddle: A working saddle, traditionally used on ranches and for working cattle, characterized by a horn at the pommel where ropes are tied.

Withers: The ridge between the horse's shoulder bones.

Wolf teeth: Teeth that appear in front of the molars. They're removed if they interfere with the bit.

Worming paste: A pasty product that comes in a tube and is squirted into a horse's mouth periodically to control internal parasites, which are one of the most common and potentially serious health problems affecting horses. If horses aren't wormed, parasites can cause a variety of problems, ranging from weight loss to anemia to deadly colic.

Index

Other Storey Titles You Will Enjoy

The Basics of Western Riding, by Charlene Strickland. Gives new riders and those crossing over from other disciplines a thorough introduction to Western riding. 160 pages. Paperback. ISBN 1-58017-030-7.

Becoming an Effective Rider, by Cherry Hill. Teaches riders how to evaluate their own skills, plan a work session, set goals and achieve them, and protect themselves from injury. 192 pages. Paperback. ISBN 0-88266-688-6.

Competing in Western Shows and Events, by Charlene Strickland. Focuses on Western horse show basics, the rules and players, showing for intermediate riders, showing your work horse, timed events, and arena exercises. 160 pages. Paperback. ISBN 1-58017-031-5.

From the Center of the Ring, by Cherry Hill. Covers all aspects of equestrian competition, both English and Western. 192 pages. Paperback. ISBN 0-88266-494-8.

Getting Your First Horse, by Judith Dutson. A comprehensive resource for first-time horse buyers. Includes information on choosing the best horse for you, boarding and care options, safety, horse health, and feeding. 176 pages. Paperback. ISBN 1-58017-078-1.

Horse Handling & Grooming: A Step-by-Step Photographic Guide, by Cherry Hill. Includes feeding, haltering, tying, grooming, clipping, bathing, braiding, and blanketing. The wealth of practical advice offered is thorough enough for beginners, yet useful enough for experienced riders improving or expanding their skills. 144 pages. Paperback. ISBN 0-88266-956-7.

Horse Health Care: A Step-by-Step Photographic Guide, by Cherry Hill. Explains bandaging, giving shots, examining teeth, deworming, exercising, and preventive care. 160 pages. Paperback. ISBN 0-88266-955-9.

Horse Sense: A Complete Guide to Horse Selection & Care, by John J. Mettler Jr. D.V.M. Provides the basics on selecting, housing, fencing, and feeding a horse, including information on immunizations, dental care, and breeding. 160 pages. Paperback. ISBN 0-88266-545-6.

101 Arena Exercises, by Cherry Hill. This unique wire-bound ringside workout book can be hung up or draped over the rail ring for easy reference. English and Western exercises are fully explained. 224 pages. Paperback. ISBN 0-88266-316-X.

Starting & Running Your Own Horse Business, by Mary Ashby McDonald. This essential guide shows readers how to run a successful business and how to make the most of their investments in horses, facilities, equipment, and time. 160 pages. Paperback. ISBN 0-88266-960-5.

Taking Up Riding as an Adult, by Diana Delmar. Provides a wealth of information, including riding for exercise and fun, selecting a lesson stable and instructor, and when it's time to buy your first horse. 160 pages. Paperback. ISBN 1-58017-081-1.

Teaching Safe Horsemanship: A Guide to English and Western Instruction, by Jan Dawson. Presents a step-by-step teaching program focusing on safety lessons, boarding, showing, and guest ranch activities. Explains protective release forms, insurance, and dealing with an accident or lawsuit. 160 pages. Hardcover. ISBN 0-88266-972-9.

These and other Storey books are available at your bookstore, farm store, garden center, or directly from Storey Books, Schoolhouse Road, Pownal, Vermont 05261, or by calling 1-800-441-5700. Or visit our website at www.storey.com.

The mission of Storey Communications is to serve our customers
by publishing practical information that encourages personal independence
in harmony with the environment.

Text development by Diana Delmar
Edited by Janet Lape and Elizabeth McHale
Cover design by Rob Johnson, Johnson Design
Front cover and interior photographs by Lisa Helfert
Back cover photograph © Jimi Akin
Text design by Faith Hague and Susan Bernier
Text production by Erin Lincourt
Illustrations by James E. Dyekman
Indexed by Susan Olason/Indexes & Knowledge Maps

Printed in Canada by Transcontinental Printing
10 9 8 7 6 5 4 3 2 1

Library of Congress Cataloging-in-Publication Data

Smith, Michael W., 1948–
    Getting the most from riding lessons / by Mike Smith
        p.   cm. — (A horse-wise guide)
    Includes index.
    ISBN 1-58017-082-X (alk. paper)
    1. Horsemanship. I. Title. II. Series.
SF309.S625 1998
798.2—DC21   98-6393
                                    CIP

Getting the
Most from
Riding Lessons

HORSE
WISE
GUIDES

Mike Smith

STOREY
BOOKS